CW00361589

27

The Royal Lyceum Theatre, Edinburgh
and the National Theatre of Scotland present

27

BY ABI MORGAN

OBERON BOOKS
LONDON

WWW.OBERONBOOKS.COM

First published in 2011 by Oberon Books Ltd
521 Caledonian Road, London N7 9RH
Tel: +44 (0) 20 7607 3637 / Fax: +44 (0) 20 7607 3629
e-mail: info@oberonbooks.com
www.oberonbooks.com

Abi Morgan is hereby identified as author of this play in
accordance with section 77 of the Copyright, Designs and Patents
Act 1988. The author has asserted her moral rights.

A catalogue record for this book is available from the British
Library.

ISBN: 978-1-84943-177-4

Cover image by Mark Hamilton

Printed and bound by CPI Group (UK) Ltd, Croydon, CR0 4YY.

27 was first performed on Tuesday 25 October 2011 at the
Royal Lyceum Theatre, Edinburgh in a co-production with the
National Theatre of Scotland.

Cast

Maureen Beattie	SISTER URSULA MARY
Emma Hartley-Miller	AUDREY MARIE
Finn den Hertog	DR SAM PARKER
Molly Innes	SISTER RUTH AUGUSTINE
Libby King	DR HELEN JARVIS
Colette O'Neil	SISTER MIRIAM THOMASINA
Nicholas Le Prevost	DR RICHARD GARFIELD
Benny Young	DR JONATHAN LEES

Creative Team

Abi Morgan	*Writer*
Vicky Featherstone	*Director*
Merle Hensel	*Set Designer*
Nick Powell	*Composer & Sound Designer*
Natasha Chivers	*Lighting Designer*
Nick Sagar	*Sound Associate*
Jenna Watt	*Assistant Director*
Anne Henderson	*Casting Director*

Characters

DR RICHARD GARFIELD *(60s)*
American, Epidemiologist, University of Alabama

DR SAM PARKER *(early/mid 30s)*
British, Epidemiologist, University of Edinburgh

DR HELEN JARVIS *(late 30s/early 40s)*
American, Neurophysiologist. University of Alabama

DR JONATHAN LEES *(early 50s)*
British, Neurologist. National Institute of Ageing

SISTER MIRIAM THOMASINA *(late 90s)*
Mother Superior

SISTER URSULA MARY *(late 40s/early 50s)*
Sister Procurator / Mother Superior

SISTER RUTH AUGUSTINE *(late 40s)*
Sister Portress

AUDREY MARIE *(early/mid 20s)*
Aspirant.

Setting

The play is set in a modern Catholic Convent somewhere in West Scotland over five years.

/ Denotes when lines intercut

Act One

An office.

A desk. A filing cabinet. Three chairs. There is a vase of roses in full bloom on the desk.

RICHARD stands, a cup of tea in his hand.

HELEN stands looking out of a distant window, distracted.

It is summer.

HELEN: Is that someone swimming?

> *RICHARD follows HELEN's gaze out of the window. HELEN takes in the room, leaning forward to look at a painting on the wall.*

MIRIAM: *'Joshua Roll'.* The original's preserved in the Vatican.

> *MIRIAM enters, ready to greet them.*

HELEN: It's beautiful.

MIRIAM: A picture is to the illiterate what the religious word is to the educated.*(Beat.)* I don't remember who it was who said that.

> *The action freezes –*

RICHARD: *(To audience.)* So this is how it started –

> *The action springs back into life –*

MIRIAM: I'm so/

RICHARD: No/

MIRIAM: …sorry. Ruth should have/

RICHARD: It's not a problem. /

MIRIAM: …told me you were here. Normally word gets around. /

RICHARD: Really… We only just arrived/

MIRIAM: Dr Garfield.

RICHARD: Please, Richard *(Introducing HELEN.)* And this is Dr Jarvis.

HELEN smiles in greeting to MIRIAM.

HELEN: Helen's just fine.

MIRIAM: …There are always whispers. How long have you been – ?

RICHARD: …five, ten minutes that's all.

MIRIAM: Really someone should have at least got you/

RICHARD: They have. They did.

RICHARD holds up a teacup.

MIRIAM: …tea. *(Beat.)* Good. *(Calling out.)* You sure you wouldn't prefer coffee? *(Beat.)*

RICHARD: Well…/

MIRIAM: I knew it. I knew it.

MIRIAM reaches for her phone, tapping buttons –

… *(As phone answers.)* Charlotte, I just called Ruth… Is she…? …Never mind. Could we have coffee please? I know but…tea is a poor cousin, Charlotte, that you should know. Thank you. Can someone please tell Ursula to come and find us seeing as she invited these guests here? And root out a digestive if we have one. You're a dear. *(As puts down the phone.)* Don't let us get away with that again. If we can't give you something decent to drink… Or would you prefer a cold drink?

RICHARD: There was talk of –

MIRIAM: It's Friday. On Friday, there's always lemonade.

A distant ripple of laughter.

(Beat.) You came –

RICHARD: Plane, then train.

MIRIAM: From Euston?

RICHARD: I think…

HELEN: Heathrow to Paddington, Paddington to Euston, Euston to –/

MIRIAM: The train must have been a nightmare/

RICHARD: …No.

MIRIAM: …for an American.

RICHARD pauses, mid sip. MIRIAM smiles, a certain mischief to her –

JONATHAN: Miriam –

Lights up on JONATHAN greeting MIRIAM enthusiastically as if he has just entered –

MIRIAM: Where have you been skulking?

JONATHAN: I was just saying to Ursula… The roses smell, wonderful… Ursula's just coming.

URSULA enters, her hair dripping wet, drying with a towel.

URSULA: I'm sorry…I'm sorry…I couldn't understand why Ruth was waving and by the time I had swum back/

MIRIAM: You're dripping.

URSULA: …I found Jonathan wandering in the garden, stealing strawberries.

JONATHAN: That river…

URSULA laughs.

URSULA: It's very low at this time of year.

URSULA holds out a handful of strawberries to JONATHAN, who takes one and eats.

URSULA: The ducks don't even try. I beat them at breaststroke.

JONATHAN: Still. You get caught in those reeds and –

URSULA: There's hardly a tug until you're down to the weir.

HELEN: I'd love a swim.

URSULA: Have one? Really it's the only thing that saves me whatever time of the day.

JONATHAN: Now have you all met?

URSULA looks to RICHARD and HELEN shaking hands in greeting.

RICHARD: We saw you from the window.

MIRIAM: She's in a world of her own. Head down, arms going, fixed on a point straight ahead.

RICHARD: I've heard so much about you.

URSULA: Jonathan? It's all flannel. He knows how to butter us up.

JONATHAN: That's not true. Ursula is Jackie to Miriam's JFK.

MIRIAM: She's my right hand. You are. She takes over at the end of the year.

URSULA: Though I'm not letting her go far.

MIRIAM: We're easing her into the job gently.

URSULA: It's a fairly new suit so I apologise before we even begin. Jonathan believes I affect this air of chaos but really –

MIRIAM: Nonsense, you'll be running this place long after I'm in the ground. Ursula's been with us since she was –

URSULA: 1970…something too long ago for me to repeat in public.

MIRIAM: She was fifteen and shaking all the way on the drive here. In artistic circles I think one would call her a protégé.

URSULA: Thank the Lord we're not in artistic circles then.

RICHARD: Fifteen. So young.

URSULA: My aunt brought me. I was practically an orphan. Thankfully, Miriam took me in.

MIRIAM: The roses are beautiful, Ursula.

URSULA: Ruth/

RUTH enters with a jug of lemonade. URSULA throws her hands up, gesturing to RUTH –

MIRIAM: At last…

URSULA: …is to be congratulated for all flower arranging.

RUTH: *(To URSULA.)* There you are. We almost sent out a search party.

MIRIAM: I asked Charlotte/

RUTH: Coffee. On its way.

MIRIAM: See, word travels.

MIRIAM takes the jug of lemonade from RUTH –

Lemonade is our consolation.

…and starts to pour.

Drink –

MIRIAM hands a glass to JONATHAN.

You're quite purple with the heat.

RUTH: There's a young man downstairs. He says his name is Dr Parker –

JONATHAN: Damn –

JONATHAN looks to RUTH, senses her quiet disapproval.

He's early. *(To RICHARD.)* Edinburgh were keen to provide one of their own. *(Beat.)* Don't give me that look, Richard. Just don't. They're funding a large slice of the study. Diplomacy is the key.

RUTH: Shall I bring him up?

MIRIAM: If you would.

MIRIAM nods, RUTH makes to go.

MIRIAM: Ruth is Sister Portress. She knows everything that comes in and goes out.

RUTH exits passing AUDREY as she enters with a pot of coffee and a tray of biscuits. URSULA swipes a biscuit in passing.

URSULA: Audrey, you're a good girl.

AUDREY: Bourbons. I couldn't find digestives.

URSULA: Remind me to write a memo to the board.

URSULA grins, sinking down into a chair, taking a cup of coffee and swiping a biscuit.

Audrey's been with us six weeks. We're trying to convince her of the virtues of a contemplative life.

AUDREY goes to put down the pot of coffee, scalding herself.

AUDREY: Ah shit!

URSULA: She's a great mind.

MIRIAM: *(To AUDREY.)* Have you seen Aileen about?

AUDREY: Downstairs, wrestling with some chickens in the kitchen. They got stuck together in the freezer. Bernice is trying to gouge them apart.

MIRIAM: Audrey, would you?

URSULA: I'll go. I'll go.

MIRIAM: Ursula –

URSULA makes to go.

URSULA: She wanted to do crab but Ruth and I convinced her that it doesn't smell like that if it's fresh. She bought them off that friend of Robert's. I've already told him not again. It's fish that's not seen sea in six months.

MIRIAM: No really. Let Audrey do it.

URSULA finishing up her tea, and exits.

(To AUDREY.) Tell her to lay for four more while you're at it.

AUDREY exits.

She's going to kill us with a chorus line of poultry…

MIRIAM shrugs, smiles.

We've had three sisters down with the runs only last week because someone didn't defrost the meat through. There was a time when we had our own livestock but – It was that or a new TV room. TV was the victor. Now it's a monthly trip to Iceland. I love it but some of the others get upset. They like meat that's had a pulse. We tell them it's organic. They're all God's creatures. That's what I console them with.

SAM enters.

JONATHAN: Here he is. Sam.

JONATHAN goes over to greet SAM.

SAM: Sorry…sorry… Sorry… –

JONATHAN shakes hands with SAM as he takes off his jacket and puts down his briefcase.

…I've been standing since Edinburgh… The heating stuck on full blast.

SAM goes to greet HELEN. HELEN smiles, wiping her hands on a tissue.

HELEN: Don't come too close. Some guy in the next seat, sat with his dog, its butt in my face.

SAM: You got an earlier train.

HELEN: I got an earlier train.

JONATHAN: You've met?

HELEN: We have.

SAM: Strasburg. Last autumn.

MIRIAM: Just fish out the lemon.

MIRIAM hands a glass of lemonade to SAM.

SAM: …Thank you… I can't quite believe I am here. *(Drinks.)* This is good.

JONATHAN: Miriam, Dr Sam Parker, a rising star in our field.

MIRIAM: We're honoured.

SAM: That's just Jonathan. He exaggerates. Thank you for having us here.

JONATHAN: And of course Dr Garfield.

JONATHAN introduces RICHARD. SAM shakes RICHARD's hand enthusiastically.

SAM: *(To RICHARD.)* We met in Berlin. I came to hear your paper/

RICHARD: I remember…

SAM: 'The Legacy of the Depressive Mind.' Your argument for pre-condition screening was very –

RICHARD: You challenged me on my figures.

SAM: …convincing.

RICHARD: *(Beat.)* I'm not a natural speaker.

JONATHAN: He lies.

RICHARD: No, really I hate those things.

JONATHAN: Your speech at/

RICHARD: That was my wedding.

JONATHAN: …was rather funny, really rather funny.

RICHARD: No one laughed.

JONATHAN: I laughed. /

RICHARD: Exactly.

JONATHAN: Beautiful wedding. We made a holiday of it. It was only –

RICHARD: Six… Seven…Yes nearly seven weeks ago now.

MIRIAM: Congratulations.

JONATHAN: It's ridiculous. Can you believe he's never been married before? Laura's – ?

RICHARD: Fine. Laura's great. We're settling into married life. She doesn't like my taste in shoes. Or cutlery. Out with the old in with the new.

JONATHAN: That woman is a saint.

RICHARD: It has been duly noted.

JONATHAN: Richard is the only man I know who takes his new bride to Leeds for her honeymoon.

RICHARD: The neurology unit had asked me to speak. *(Beat.)* We saw a castle…

JONATHAN: A castle. *(Beat.)* How terrifically romantic. *(To MIRIAM.)* Sam will be overseeing the study and assisting the UK arm of the project, shadowing Richard.

URSULA enters, with a smile.

URSULA: The poultry are parted. Dinner might be a little late. So if anyone needs a snack. Aileen's up for making sandwiches.

SAM: The view is/

RICHARD: …stunning.

URSULA: Yes.

JONATHAN smiles, gesturing to SAM.

JONATHAN: Ursula? Sam?

URSULA: Yes, we crossed on the stairs.

URSULA follows RICHARD's gaze, looking out.

Do you have a view, Dr Garfield?

RICHARD: No. I have a wall.

URSULA: That can also be…

MIRIAM: We should get started. Only time is…

URSULA: Sorry. Sorry. *(Beat.)* You just have to tell me to shut up.

URSULA closes the door, goes to sit but instead pours herself another cup of coffee. She holds up the pot to RICHARD.

URSULA: More coffee?

RICHARD shakes his head.

It'll be my fifth of the day, although apparently, there is just as much, if not more caffeine, in your average cup of Earl Grey.

MIRIAM looks at URSULA.

…Silence.

JONATHAN: *(To RICHARD.)* Will you?

RICHARD: If you prefer.

JONATHAN: I would.

RICHARD: Ok… *(Beat.)* Sister –

MIRIAM: Miriam.

RICHARD: Miriam, you'll have already heard of our work in the States, I think Jonathan sent you some papers –/

MIRIAM: Yes.

RICHARD: My apologies, if you found them a little dry.

MIRIAM: I confess they defeated me somewhat.

JONATHAN: I'm pushing for them to publish but Richard believes –

RICHARD: Despite Jonathan's best efforts, we've managed to keep it pretty quiet so far.

Beat.

The study's in its ninth year, working across seven of the mid-Western states. Your sisters in the US have been very generous with their time.

URSULA: We're in contact with our sisters in Missouri. Only last August. Sister Loretta/

RICHARD: …Sister Loretta Hope is a particular favourite.

URSULA: …She's a marvel. Her letters are a hoot. The last one detailed how she built a BBQ. She did all the brickwork herself. And she's 89 –

RICHARD: 89.

URSULA: Did you know she's doing a masters in Islam?

RICHARD: I didn't.

URSULA: We'd be hard pushed to match them though Sister Mary Jane Brody hits her 103rd birthday this September and she can do every word on *Countdown*.

MIRIAM: Ursula.

URSULA: Am I doing it again? Sorry. Words just spill with me.

URSULA takes a seat, determinedly silent. RICHARD smiles.

RICHARD: I'm not exactly sure what Jonathan has told you./

JONATHAN: I thought it would be better if the sisters hear the core of the proposal from you.

RICHARD: As head of the Institute of Ageing, I know that Jonathan has been visiting you. The institute's US arm has provided a large proportion of our funding. *(Beat.)* We're already talking to your sister convent in – .

URSULA: …Aberdeen. We had a call last week.

RICHARD: Jonathan may have mentioned we've met a little resistance so far.

JONATHAN: The key is someone leading, someone seen to be leading the way –

MIRIAM: Jonathan, you're jumping around like a grasshopper.

JONATHAN: Sorry. Sorry…I just thought… Sorry –

JONATHAN sits, drinks his coffee.

…It drives my wife mad.

RICHARD: We're keen to establish a second study in the UK. To build upon what we've already learnt in the US. *(Beat.)* We need to find at least 200 willing candidates. You currently have 16 –

MIRIAM: 17. If you consider Audrey.

RICHARD: 13 of those sisters are in the relevant age bracket.

MIRIAM: Age bracket?

RICHARD: *(Beat.)* He hasn't told you a thing.

JONATHAN: Not exactly. Not entirely. I wanted the whole team to be here today to answer any questions you may have.

RICHARD: *(Beat.)* Our study sisters range from 75 to 106. Thirteen of your sisters are in the relevant age bracket to participate in our study. With the fourteen at your sister convent, we would have 27 potential candidates in total in the UK so far. In particular we're interested in the effect of ageing on the human mind and developing our understanding of what constitutes a healthy life.

JONATHAN: You're getting all of this, OK, Miriam?

MIRIAM: Yes, Jonathan, thank you, Dr Garfield's English is surprisingly good.

JONATHAN: I'm just ensuring everyone is up to speed…

URSULA: Absolutely.

JONATHAN: It's just –

URSULA: We're fine.

RICHARD: For an epidemiologist like myself, your religious order provides the ideal study group. Your lives have been carefully regulated. Copious records have been maintained. ...To be frank as a community you're easy to track. The noviciate autobiographies alone –

MIRIAM: Yes?

RICHARD: ...are very exciting to us. A detailed insight to a sister's early life, a biography written in as an aspirant about to take her vows which we can use to compare language skills, idea density with that of the same sister today. *(Beat.)* In particular we're trying to further our understanding of Alzheimer's in the ageing mind.

JONATHAN: It's a very attractive proposition, Miriam. The Institute would of course make some kind of covenant, a bi-yearly donation of some kind.

MIRIAM: You want to work here?

URSULA: Now wait and hear what they have to say.

JONATHAN: Richard's team would monitor the physical and mental effects of ageing through a series of simple well-established tests.

URSULA pours herself another cup of coffee, watching MIRIAM. JONATHAN holds out his cup.

MIRIAM: Tests?

JONATHAN: Sam?

SAM: These are called MMSE or mini-mental state exams.

JONATHAN: They're approved by the National Institute of Ageing in both America and over here.

HELEN: They're designed to assess verbal fluency, word recognition etc.

RICHARD: This is Helen's particular area of expertise. They offer some kind of prognosis. It's not a definitive analysis of Alzheimer's per se but –

JONATHAN: All findings remain confidential, known only to the sister if she wishes.

Silence. URSULA looks to MIRIAM, sees she is clearly struggling.

We appreciate this might be a lot to take in in one go.

MIRIAM: 'Exam'. The word 'exam' is –

SAM: …misleading.

MIRIAM: Most of our sisters haven't taken any kind of qualification since their masters or teaching diplomas. Many of them have found vocation in say the garden or the kitchen. Any kind of exam –

RICHARD: …certainly don't compare. The last thing I want to inflict are exams on anyone. I was the worst student in my class.

MIRIAM: Still. Then what are they?

HELEN: They're small exercises, almost like games to stimulate and assess processing, language or let's say memory skills, designed to create some kind of criteria to examine levels of physical and mental coherence.

SAM: They last no more than an hour over two days, and are carried out on a yearly basis. This is then compared with the pathology of a sister after –

JONATHAN: Sam –

MIRIAM: After? *(Beat.)* Ursula?

RICHARD: This is a very sensitive request…

URUSLA: They want our brains.

JONATHAN: Tissue.

RICHARD: One can't deny this is a highly provocative – /

URSULA: Our sister convent will agree if we do as well.

MIRIAM: Right.

URSULA takes another biscuit, eats.

RICHARD: The co-operation of the sisters in America has been dependent on their benevolence and genuine belief in our work. The donation is essential for those agreeing to participate in the study.

URSULA: *(Eats.)* I'm eating all these bourbons.

URSULA puts down the biscuit. JONATHAN shifts in his chair as RUTH enters with more coffee.

RUTH: Aileen was asking if anyone's vegetarian.

JONATHAN: We're weren't expecting supper.

MIRIAM: We can't not feed you, now you're here.

RICHARD goes to speak but hesitates on seeing RUTH still loitering.

Everything alright Ruth?

RUTH: Yes… Sorry.

MIRIAM: No vegetarians I think.

Silence. MIRIAM looks to RUTH waiting for her to go until –

URSULA: Ruth is a trained nurse.

RICHARD: Really?

RUTH nods, letting the silence hang.

URSULA: She's read a lot about your work in America.

MIRIAM: *(To RUTH.)* You have?

RUTH: Ursula and I talked a little.

URSULA: She's a demon with her articles. Let her loose amongst the broadsheets with a pair of scissors…

RUTH: It seems very interesting… Your study I mean?

RICHARD: We're hoping so.

URSULA: She worked in Africa.

RUTH: It was years ago. *(Beat.)* I aided some of the smallpox vaccination programmes for a little while in Eastern Africa and the Niger through most of the late 80s.

RICHARD: Then you must understand more than most –

RUTH: …the benefits of such work. Yes.

RUTH starts to pile cups on a tray, MIRIAM waits. RUTH nods, making to go.

MIRIAM: So you'll let Aileen know?

RUTH nods then exits.

How many have you so far? *(Beat.)* Donations?

RICHARD: There are 700 sisters participating in the programme in the US. 128 have passed away since we started in '97. Of which actual tissue donations are 49. We allow for a certain number of sisters to drop out nearer the time due to family wishes or through a change of heart of some kind. We would need tissue… Plus unlimited access to all noviciate autobiographies, medical records and relevant documentation held on each sister participating. *(Beat.)* As Jonathan mentioned, your sister convents in the UK, have certain reservations but –

JONATHAN: If you were seen to be leading the way/

MIRIAM: We've had a recent rise in the popularity of the open casket –

JONATHAN: It's a very simple procedure.

RICHARD: The sisters would still be able to be viewed even after –

MIRIAM: That sorts that one then.

MIRIAM absently follows the sound of footsteps, of someone passing.

URSULA: Miriam?

MIRIAM: *(Beat.)* The brain is not just –

RICHARD: …an organ of the body, no.

MIRIAM: The brain –

RICHARD: Yes.

MIRIAM: …it's the very essence of being, of who we are.

RICHARD: Yes I can see that.

SAM: *(Beat.)* Richard, do you mind if I?

RICHARD hesitates, nods. SAM takes a seat opposite MIRIAM.

No one underestimates what we're asking you to consider. But does it help if I tell you that in the last nine years, it's widely believed Dr Garfield's work has come closer to answering some of the fundamental questions on brain degeneration than any other study currently being undertaken…

RICHARD: You're being a little too kind.

JONATHAN: Ssh.

SAM: Why is it that one sister ages gracefully, all faculties in tact through into late life often passing her centenary and yet another, who has lived a comparable in many cases almost identical life in terms of education, socialisation, medical care, nutrition, lifestyle, seem to lose herself with a steady degeneration of her mental faculties? A sister who can't recognise her own family or even what time of day it is and yet whose life has been identical to that of the other?

JONATHAN: Sam's unit of memory and ageing at Edinburgh are doing some very interesting research on folic acid, its beneficial effect on the brain in early life.

SAM: We're hanging on the US' coat tails. But in Richard's work…I genuinely believe he will find a cure.

RICHARD: That's not strictly –

JONATHAN: Do you think Louis Pasteur could afford to be this modest?

RICHARD: Understanding, understanding will suit me fine.

MIRIAM: What do you think, Ursula?

URSULA: I told you we should eat more liver. That's packed with folic acid. We eat the odd takeaway burger, but don't go spreading that around. It breaks up the nun run from town and back.

JONATHAN: You're not taking this seriously.

URSULA tidies the last of the things on the tray, going to take JONATHAN's cup.

I know how important your opinion is to Miriam.

URSULA: *(Beat.)* I am just heir in waiting.

JONATHAN: Nonsense you are the rock star of the
ecclesiastical world.

MIRIAM laughs.

URSULA: And now you're encouraging him.

JONATHAN: It's true.

URSULA looks to MIRIAM, sensing her waiting.

URSULA: Most of them will take their lead from you. You've
run this place since God began…

MIRIAM: You invited them here.

URSULA: They made their vow of obedience to you.

MIRIAM: And soon to you.

URSULA hesitates, pouring herself more coffee.

JONATHAN: Now take your time – Really don't be rushed on
this.

URSULA: No. You don't want to catch us on a different day.

MIRIAM: How many of us would it affect?

RICHARD: Thirteen here. 27 in total.

URSULA: But with time –

RICHARD: You're a long way off being old enough for our
study.

URSULA: I'll hold on to mine a little longer then.

HELEN: In some of the convents we've visited, the sisters have
put it to a ballot. We've found it can be very helpful in
uniting these communities.

MIRIAM: These communities?

Distant sound of bells.

I presume you'd want to start quite soon.

RICHARD: We'd monitor the sisters on a yearly basis. The time
varies, it could be summer it could be the fall. Dr Jarvis

and I would conduct the assessment here over say a two week period.

HELEN: We would clinically examine the sisters as well as conducting the tests with our team. This data along with all other documentation kept through their lives is collated and stored on our computers. Following death the data would then be definitively compared to assess where there is a correlation with MMSEs scoring, the other forms of testing and changes in the brain tissue.

RICHARD: The American Psychiatric association have laid out detailed guidelines to distinguish non-Alzheimer's dementia from possible or probable Alzheimer's but there is no definitive test, no scan, no blood test that can provide absolute certainty until after death.

MIRIAM: Whatever the sisters may be to you, to us they are still very much in the living.

RICHARD: No one doubts that.

URSULA: We were born to serve our fellow man, I can't think of a better way of helping him, Miriam.

MIRIAM: You decide.

URSULA looks to MIRIAM.

You invited them here, Ursula.

A beat.

URSULA: A ballot it is. Though it would be best to address the sisters straight after supper. They have an hour's recreation at 7.30 and you would be advised to get in before their soaps start. For some the order of *Eastenders* carries greater comfort than a whole evening of prayer. If we over run, I'll hide the remote, that normally foxes them.

The bell passes as if moving just past MIRIAM's office.

You can amuse yourself for the next hour? Audrey will show you around if you like. We still have the gardens in full working order. August is the best time, there's plums if you can find them and of course if you fancy a dip in the weir.

MIRIAM goes to exit.

MIRIAM: The necessary arrangements would be put in place by you in the event of a death of a consenting sister?

RICHARD: Yes.

SAM: The brain would be removed, boxed and posted and be on a lab slide within six weeks.

JONATHAN and RICHARD both turn to look at SAM.

JONATHAN: Christ, Sam.

SAM: Sorry…sorry.

URSULA: You might want to phrase it a different way once you get in there. One or two of them are a bit queasy and they would've been even more so if Aileen hadn't got those chickens apart.

RICHARD: Four million people in America currently suffer from Alzheimer's disease. There will be 7.7 million by the year 2030. There will be 115 million by 2050, worldwide.

MIRIAM: That's a lot of lost people.

MIRIAM goes to exit. SAM, HELEN and JONATHAN follow. URSULA goes to tidy the last of the tea things, following RICHARD's gaze, looking outside.

URSULA: Go to the weir if you can make it. This time of day, it's the quietest place you'll find around here. Everyone's always surprised how noisy it is when they visit. You're never really ever alone, even if you wanted to be.

URSULA exits. RICHARD stands, the cup still in his hand.

RICHARD: *(To audience.)* A healthy adult female brain usually weighs between 1,100 and 1,400 grams. That's about 2-3lbs in old money. Hold it in your hand and you soon appreciate the weight of this gift, feel it. The brain of most Alzheimer's patients is noticeably smaller. They often shrink below 1,000 grams, as the disease destroys the brain tissue. You become adept at knowing this just by looking.

As you lift it out of the box, already telling you something. The surface already confirming or destroying what you thought you'd already had pinned down. Like a beautiful landscape that you've painted in your mind though you've never actually been to. Now you get to visit, to see all its ruts and curves and valleys, the odd rogue crevasse that you hadn't expected to find. You get to photograph it and slice it and hold it up to the light and look at it under a microscope. You know the person it belonged to. You probably laughed with them over a game of scrabble, or been surprised when after weeks of blind staring in the corner of some convent hallway, they wink at you. Like the first smile of a baby, delightful. As if they're saying 'Hey there is someone in here, everything is still firing, just maybe in a slower gear.' You've got all of it, right there. I think of it as my friend. I think of it as someone I once knew. I think of it as the key to the most secret part of someone's life, and that someone has left that key with me. And I'm grateful. I'm always grateful. But it's still a weight, an ever present weight, just there, a constant in my hand.

RICHARD puts down the coffee cup, sliding it onto the tray.

Act Two

A library.

A long table. Chairs. A low wide bowl of pomegranates on the table.

HELEN sits working, talking into a Dictaphone, reading from a pile of documents in front of her –

It is winter, three years on. 2009.

HELEN: *(Reading/into Dictaphone.)* I was born in Greenock. Though my da was a Corkman. Eleven words. Punctuated on the fifth and the eleventh word – End. Note to self predominately monosyllabic bar the colloquial noun 'da'. I was one of six. Two boys and four girls, a seventh, Michael died in childbirth. Five. Five. Two. Punctuation – Comma. Two. Punctuation – Comma. Five. Punctuation – Full stop.

HELEN takes notes throughout, talking into a Dictaphone –

MIRIAM: Am I in the way?

HELEN smiles, flicks off her Dictaphone.

HELEN: No.

MIRIAM: Don't be shy to say.

HELEN: Really Miriam. It's fine.

MIRIAM nods. HELEN resumes working, turning the Dictaphone back on.

(Reading/into Dictaphone.) I was one of six. Two boys and four girls, a seventh, Michael died in childbirth.

SAM enters, sinking on seeing MIRIAM.

MIRIAM: Sam, now you promised me…

HELEN smiles, amused –

SAM: Rats! Found.

MIRIAM holds up the lamp.

SAM: I swear you save these jobs up for me.

SAM goes in search of a socket, plugging them in. Nothing.

MIRIAM: Yes I do. I think it's the plug.

MIRIAM hands him a screwdriver.

And can you try and mend my desk lamp after, please. It's on then it's off, as if one is under visitation from a poltergeist.

HELEN smiles, resumes working.

HELEN: *(Reading/into Dictaphone.)* Five. Five. Two. Punctuation – Comma. Two. Punctuation – Comma. Five. Punctuation – Full stop.

HELEN hesitates, aware of MIRIAM hovering close by. She flicks off the Dictaphone, works on.

MIRIAM: It's a foreign language.

HELEN: It's pretty impenetrable.

MIRIAM: Though linguistics has always been a passion.

MIRIAM peers over HELEN's shoulder, reading.

HELEN: Please. I give a scoring every ten or so words based on grammatical complexity –

MIRIAM: I see, yes.

HELEN: Richness of vocabulary,

MIRIAM: Fascinating.

HELEN: Density of ideas and positive or negative emotion –

MIRIAM: Searching for the embedded clauses.

HELEN watching MIRIAM, absorbed in reading.

HELEN: Exactly. The verb phrase infinitive complexes, incidents of repetition and anaphora…

MIRIAM: Anaphora.

HELEN: Reading them is like striking gold. Whole lives, so perfectly notated, really. It never fails to humble me.

MIRIAM: Yes, words do last, yet what they say is not always the same. For example Anaphora, a rhetorical device, rhetoric. A referential pattern in linguistics… Yes… Then there is Anaphora…part of the divine liturgy in Eastern Christianity.

MIRIAM watches HELEN working. MIRIAM looks over her shoulder again reading.

And what one writes as a young woman one perceives as something so entirely different I find…with time…with age.

MIRIAM moves across the room.

HELEN: It's quite a library you have down there.

MIRIAM: We're very lucky. We've built it up over the years.

HELEN: A real legacy.

MIRIAM: *(Beat.)* That's something then.

HELEN: I've been trying to teach Audrey. It's laborious I know but if she knows the phrases when she types them up then it will make life a lot easier, for her. It's all useful experience for her resume.

MIRIAM looks at her bemused.

For when she works outside?

MIRIAM: Is Audrey leaving?

HELEN: I don't…know…I just meant.

MIRIAM: She arrived here in quite a state. She'd not had a bath in two months. A bed maybe longer. She'll leave when she wants to.

HELEN: And if she stays?

MIRIAM peers at a book on the shelf.

MIRIAM: *Playboy of the Western World.* What a play!

MIRIAM takes it out of the shelf, considers, smiling to herself.

JM Synge. Have you ever seen it?

HELEN: No.

MIRIAM: Neither have I. But we've read it. Time and time again. Before we had a television.

HELEN clocks MIRIAM's cardigan, the label visible at the base of her neck as she walks away.

Ursula and I.

MIRIAM smiles, looks over HELEN's shoulder.

Such dedication.

MIRIAM smiles, makes to go –

HELEN: You have your cardigan on inside out?

MIRIAM: Hmm.

MIRIAM feels for a label, laughs –

Oh yes, so I do –

MIRIAM points a finger at SAM before she exits.

MIRIAM: I will be back.

MIRIAM exits. SAM looks to HELEN.

SAM: A catalogue of little jobs every time I sit down to start work.

HELEN: I'm not saying anything.

SAM: I mean why do they even employ Robert?

HELEN: He lives with his mother and it gives him a chance to get out.

SAM: You speak to him?

HELEN: I'm very fond of Robert.

SAM: Fond is not a word I'd associate with you.

AUDREY enters carrying a pile of files, heading towards HELEN.

AUDREY: Biscuit, table, airplane, handbag, dog, envelope, policeman, lake, pencil… I know it…I know it…

SAM reaches one hand across a desk and holds up a card with the word 'tambourine' on it.

AUDREY: Tambourine. …I would have got that.

AUDREY laughs, snatching the card off SAM. HELEN looks up, clearly irritated to be disturbed.

Sorry… Sorry. Those ready to go up.

HELEN nods.

HELEN: I was just telling Miriam how hard you've been working learning all the terms. To help you later.

AUDREY starts sorting through the files, putting them into different piles.

Don't you want to be able to work outside?

AUDREY: I have work.

HELEN: I thought it was a 'vocation'.

AUDREY: Aspirant. I'm an aspirant.

HELEN: Still –

AUDREY: You make it sound like a prison. Inside, outside, I can still go out. I drive the van sometimes.

HELEN: Audrey, I'm sorry I –

AUDREY: I'd rather be here than slaving in some office, trying to get a bigger house, a bigger car, ending up divorced and lonely and –

HELEN stops her note taking. AUDREY hesitates.

HELEN: *(Beat.)* I just think you're too young –

AUDREY: I'm 24 next March. *(Beat.)* Ursula thinks I could… I'm going to take a Higher next month. *(Beat.)* It's better than being smacked out nicking scratch cards all your life.

AUDREY scoops up another pile of files.

That to go up?

HELEN nods.

Is this Aileen's?

HELEN nods, catching on AUDREY looking at the file.

You know I found her. She was blue. Must have been dead ages. It's shaken them all up a bit. 78's not a bad age but she's one of the youngest. They were all checking their pulses that day.

HELEN: A stroke's a stroke.

AUDREY: She used to eat double cream frozen, straight out of the bag. Heart must have been like a sponge of fat. But God I miss her pies. Sister Maria Angelica is a f'ecking awful cook. I mean Aileen was bad but Maria…

SAM and HELEN look to one another, smile. HELEN slides a pile of files towards AUDREY.

AUDREY nods, scooping them up, making to go.

AUDREY: I didn't mean you. Divorced and lonely.

HELEN hesitates, smiles.

Sam, would you talk to Ursula because we're still using that crap PC. It took me months to type the biographies last time.

SAM: I think Jonathan might have sorted that.

AUDREY: He hasn't.

SAM: Looks like an Apple Mac to me. Of course I can't be sure because it's still inside the box, waiting in the hall for someone with a modicum of computer literacy to open it but… Think of it as an early Christmas present.

AUDREY: Hallelujah!

AUDREY is gone.

HELEN: You're flirting.

SAM: I'm not flirting…much.

SAM peers over HELEN's shoulder, close, teasing her.

So it came through at last.

HELEN: Signed the paper's August.

SAM: How is George?

HELEN: He took the cat. *(Beat.)* It's fine. I hate the cat. So does he. So he either took it as an act of selfless love, or an act of mean-minded revenge, thinking I cared… This and other irritations dog my day. How's Elizabeth?

SAM smiles, HELEN smiles, both dangerously close.

URSULA: Samuel.

URSULA enters. She is carrying a mug of coffee, and a pile of books. A plate of cake rests on top.

There you are. Ruth said you were helping out with the decorations and I find you hiding up here. Where were you this morning? You promised me. I was up early and –

SAM: I nearly drowned last Christmas –

URSULA: And the year before that.

SAM: I swam. It was August. November, you need a ice pick. There are icebergs.

URSULA: The Norwegians –

SAM: See you said that last year and I figured the Norwegians have saunas.

URSULA: …find it very good for the circulation. You're a big disappointment.

SAM: You build a sauna…?

URSULA: Now that would get them talking. When are you going to get a new suit?

SAM: As soon as someone starts paying me more.

URSULA: I will talk to Richard. Who is normally here. It's a waste of good coffee.

URSULA slides a cup of coffee down.

HELEN: I'll have it.

URSULA: Don't.

HELEN drinks winces.

HELEN: Wow. He likes his sugar.

URSULA: I've tried cutting it down, but he sniffs it out if you put in less than four spoons. Was Miriam just here?

HELEN: Yes.

HELEN barely looks up from her work. SAM tinkers with the plug on the lamp.

URSULA: I don't know why you changed it all around. August was always great, it was the best time for you to come but November. It's cold and damp and…a nothing month –

HELEN: Orders from above. They want us to work faster.

URSULA: They'll have you clocking in and out next.

HELEN: Richard's trying to keep them at bay but Jonathan is hovering eager. He's excited by the results we're getting. We all are.

SAM tinkers some more with the lamp, then plugs it in. It turns on.

URSULA: And that is why we look forward to you coming every year.

SAM: A loose bulb fitting. I'd like to take the credit for more.

SAM unplugs the lamp, making to go.

URSULA: Rumour has it you've been published.

SAM: Someone has to get us out there… It was nothing…

HELEN: That's not what Richard says.

SAM: He's read it?

URSULA: It was four columns more than Dr Kaufmann and cirrhosis of the liver. Ruth pinned it up on the notice board.

SAM makes to go, hesitating as he passes HELEN.

SAM: Can I borrow these? I want to compare the Braak scores.

HELEN scours through her pile of documents.

SAM takes them.

HELEN: If Richard finds you doing that –

SAM: Richard doesn't need to know.

URSULA: Are you going downstairs?

SAM stops mid step, cornered.

The radiator? It's that beast of a thing in the hallway.

SAM: Next time I am charging.

URSULA busies herself, tidying books back into the shelves.

URSULA: Don't mind me.

HELEN resumes talking into her Dictaphone.

HELEN: *(Reading/into Dictaphone.)* 'The sisters of Poor Clare were running the church school. Come fourteen, my Aunt, Tattie Pol as we were calling her, got us a place.'

URSULA hovers, searching for a book.

Sixteen. Punctuation – Comma. Eleven. Punctuation – Full stop. Note to self, simplistic idea density, left-sided branching, 2-3 g.c. score –

HELEN resumes reading.

(Reading/into Dictaphone.) Tattie Pol said I must. My ma's mind was gone and my da's was close behind.

HELEN hesitates.

A terrible sickness, that left them both lost for reason or words. Ma was gone 19th May 1964.

HELEN hesitates, the Dictaphone still running. HELEN suddenly flicks the Dictaphone off.

URSULA: Raphael.

URSULA holds up the book she is reading, deflects.

It's an ongoing love affair. I don't know what it is about his frescoes but I just…

HELEN nods, lost in reading, flicking the Dictaphone back on.

HELEN: *(Reading/into Dictaphone.)* I made a visit to Da a week after for he was housed now at the Landsdowne Infirmary. He howls when he sees us, and would not stop that I was a wicked girl and no good would come of me and that he was wanting his own little daughter back though I says it was me, Geraldine to him twice.

HELEN slides the Dictaphone down on the desk, still running, searching through the files, looking for something.

URSULA: Have you lost something?

HELEN: I asked Audrey for all the sisters pre 1945 so I don't know quite why this one –

HELEN holds up the document in her hand.

(Reading.) Geraldine. February 9th 1971. Way out.

URSULA: Audrey must have –

HELEN: Yes.

URSULA: Mixed up the batch or –

URSULA reaches across for the file, HELEN is working on.

I'll put it back.

HELEN snaps the document shut in her hand, resisting.

HELEN: No…you're fine. I'll do it later.

URSULA: Post 1945, we've moved to the basement, you shouldn't have that. I can take it down.

HELEN gently places a hand over the file, stopping URSULA from taking it.

HELEN: Really. It's fine.

URSULA shrugs, conceding defeat, resuming her search.

URSULA: A picture is to the illiterate what the religious word is to the educated. Pope St Gregory.

HELEN: Miriam?

URSULA: She had a terrible cold, last month. She took to her bed for four weeks. She still thinks she runs the place, and now with the wheeze on her chest.

HELEN: I was looking at her file only yesterday. Her writings are quite brilliant.

HELEN goes through the files, pulling out a particular document.

Every time we visit, I find myself pulling out her noviciate biography again, just to have a look. There's a level of vocabulary, grammatical complexity and density of ideas that is quite extraordinary –

URSULA: The 'contemplative' life certainly ekes out time and space, to educate the mind.

HELEN: I don't doubt that but… Where is it?

HELEN rewinds the Dictaphone.

Miriam's the morning after she's taken her vows –

the sun rose through my window, casting its glorious light across my bedspread, my wall was patterned with a heavenly glow that the less rigorous minded might have taken as a sign. My preference is that I need no divine intervention for this is the start of the rest of my life.

HELEN stops the tape.

HELEN: It's pure poetry. We're discovering, the early notes are a good marker, the reserves of the brain have perhaps been built in very early life. Miriam has clearly had an expansive vocabulary from early age.

URSULA: Her mother was very educated, she read a lot. I think there was a lot of healthy debate.

Beat.

URSULA: Her cold. It's left her a little scattered.

HELEN: Even so. Her tests were fine last year, though slightly less good than the year before. I will be curious how she is this time.

URSULA stands awkward, the last of her pile of books in her hand.

URSULA: T.S. Eliot.

URSULA goes to return the small poetry book.

It's signed…

HELEN takes the book.

People leave bequests.

HELEN flicks through –

We didn't have a single book in our house except the bible, though half of it was missing and the odd sports journal my father would bring home. He was brought up by my aunt, she was the religious one, she didn't approve of 'literature'. If it wasn't in the name of our Lord then it was ungodly to her. That was twaddle Miriam said, and I was to banish that thought if I was ever to open my mind to anything. There is nothing more godly than 'literature' … *'If ever you want him, just look, you'll find him on every page.'* Though to be frank, there's a couple of Henry James down there in the library where he's a bit sparse. Sister Bernice has a sweet tooth, she slips them in when she thinks we're not looking mixing up the Barbara Taylor Bradfords. I don't think it does much harm but –

RICHARD enters, RUTH close behind.

RICHARD: We're on a mass exodus from Siberia. Even the tea in our mugs is freezing over.

URSULA: Ruth has the right idea.

RUTH close behind in gloves and scarf, clutching a pile of papers, pen in hand.

You should at least wear a scarf. Promise me you got your flu jab this year.

RICHARD: I did.

URSULA: Flu jab in August and –

RICHARD: Not even a cough.

HELEN: You'll be making him soup next.

URSULA: That was Aileen's domain.

RICHARD: Are we good to stay?

RICHARD looks to HELEN, hovering.

I can't ask the sisters to sit down there much longer.

HELEN: Oh…yeah, that's fine…I want to finish up the last of the reading in my room anyway.

HELEN clears her things, scooping up her documents.

Though can I catch you later – ? Say five?

RICHARD: Five should be –

HELEN slides the file across to RICHARD in passing.

HELEN: I found you something. Try and take a look at it. Geraldine. 1971.

HELEN exits.

RICHARD takes it and starts to read until –

URSULA: Cake.

RICHARD looks up from reading, as if realising something to see –

URSULA holds out the plate of cake to RICHARD.

RICHARD: Cake is good. We don't get cake…

URSULA: Laura told me –

RICHARD: You've been talking –

URSULA: …that you cut out carbohydrates.

RICHARD: *(To RUTH.)* This woman, this woman talks to my wife more than I do.

URSULA: She also said –

RICHARD: I stop at dairy. I cannot not eat dairy.

URSULA: …That you are sneaking cheeseburgers at the weekends and that she hasn't seen you since –

RICHARD: I've been working late.

URSULA: You must be nice to her. Otherwise she'll leave you Richard, then where will you be? *(Beat.)* She called on the main phone. I told her you'd call her back. Why don't you ever pick up your phone? *(Beat.)* There is only so often that you are taking a walk outside.

URSULA holds out a plate of cake out to RICHARD.

And then we had the American –

RICHARD: American?

URSULA: I think they make aspirin or something. I do not remember. I told him he had the wrong extension –

RICHARD: You're remarkable, Ursula do you know that?

RUTH: Shall I bring Miriam up now? She's wandering around a bit lost. Sister Anna Maria was going to go first, but it might be better if we see Miriam. I know that there was some work she wanted to do in the garden later.

URSULA: I would skip Miriam this year.

RICHARD: Really?

URSULA: She's not been herself this last month.

RUTH: It was just a cold.

URSULA: I know but I really don't think she is at her best. I don't think it would be fair. In fact I think she would be relieved if you did not test her this time.

RUTH: That's not what she says.

URSULA: You talked to her?

RUTH: Dr Garfield. I think Dr Garfield had a word.

URSULA: You did?

RICHARD: She seemed fine.

URSULA: It might have just been a cold but it was evil.

RUTH: That was six weeks ago.

URSULA: It's exhausted her. And it was four weeks.

RUTH: Six. It was six weeks ago.

URSULA hesitates, looking to RUTH, quietly challenged. URSULA shrugs, smiles.

URSULA: Still. She's not been right.

RUTH: I was saying to Dr Garfield about our concerns.

URSULA: She's just tired, Ruth.

RUTH: No Ursula.

URSULA: Ruth and I will now disagree.

RUTH: I am simply saying that we need to acknowledge –

URSULA: There is nothing wrong with Miriam.

Silence.

I hope she's been behaving herself.

RICHARD: Exemplary.

URSULA: No religious literature or tracts from our favourite saints left lying around?

RICHARD: I don't think you can count the odd copy of *Private Eye*.

RUTH: Why must you two tease me so?

URSULA: Because it's so much fun.

RUTH: Have you ever had to question my work, Dr Garfield?

URSULA: For the love of God, Ruth, it's Richard's third year here. Robert is Robert. Sam is Sam. Even Mr Hadlow the butcher is Mick. You can call him Richard.

RICHARD: I could not manage without you Ruth.

RUTH: Thank you...Richard.

URSULA: You know your visits save her don't you? *(Seeing RUTH's look.)* What? The other 351 days of the year you are polishing the knocker on that front door so many times, it's ready to march itself off to a more upmarket location.

RUTH: I keep myself busy.

URSULA: Oh yes, we're all so busy doing nothing.

RUTH: It's not nothing, Ursula.

Silence.

Every day is our prayer to Christ.

URSULA: Did you read Sam's article? Eight columns. Not bad. Though it's yours I'm waiting for.

RICHARD: I promise when I think there is something worth saying, you will be first person who will read it.

URSULA: Thank you, Dr Garfield. Even so you should read Sam's.

RICHARD: I'll look it up.

RUTH suddenly pulls an article out of her pocket, handing it to RICHARD.

RUTH: It displays some of the study's best work.

RICHARD flicks a hand into his top pocket, pulling out his glasses ready to read.

The metaphor of the brain as the placemat at life's table, I thought that was quite brilliant.

RICHARD: *(As reads.)* Yes... Yes I can see that.

RUTH: It's the discovery of miracle that I was just sorry he didn't flag up.

RICHARD looks up from the article, taking in RUTH's obvious delight.

RUTH: I mean as the article says. May I?

RUTH holds out her hands, RICHARD returning the article.

RUTH: Sister Philomena... Last time you were in Missouri... I remember you all talking of this that she was translating... the letters of...here it is.

RICHARD: Poor Clare into English from the French.

RUTH: According to this she scored near perfect on both her physical and mental MMSEs. I mean Sam says here that some of the assistant sisters used to try and shuffle the cards up a little just to try and catch her out but –

RICHARD: Yes, her mind was one of the smartest and most alert we'd come across until the day she died.

RUTH: And yet, in autopsy the pathology of her brain revealed a surprising fact. *(Reading.)* Sister Philomena was marked as a Braak stage VI an absolute confirmation of severe Alzheimer's pathology based on your methods of diagnosis. Death revealed that her brain was severely damaged and yet in life...

RUTH smiles, almost elated.

She was still teaching elementary class well into her 80s.

RICHARD: She also had an abundance of grey matter, formed by the cell bodies of neurons in the neocortex. 90 per cent more than we had seen in any other sister.

RUTH: Her brain was damaged, severely damaged and yet she passed all your tests with flying colours?

RICHARD: Yes.

RUTH: It's a miracle.

RICHARD hesitates, smiles.

RICHARD: I like to think it's a miracle that we haven't found the answer to yet.

RUTH: I understand you believe that your work may one day find a cure for Alzheimer's. That's commendable. But this need for science to colonise this miracle for itself... Don't you ever think that just maybe there is no scientific answer, that the answer is God's work?

RUTH looks back over the article.

These *'escapees'* that you refer to –

URSULA: Ruth.

RUTH: Ursula does not agree with me that's why she's interrupting.

URSULA: I'm not. I am. *(Beat.)* I'm sorry. *(To RICHARD.)* Ruth is about to highlight a difference of opinion.

RUTH: I mean three years here and in America, you've been working for how long –

RICHARD: Twelve years...

RUTH: Twelve years over in America and you still don't have a scientific answer for these phenomena?

RICHARD: *(Beat.)* Nothing concrete –

RUTH: So you have no answer?

URSULA: Ruth, the Catholic Church has had centuries of miraculous occasion that we've laid claim to. We can afford to have one or two challenged.

RUTH: I'm asking Richard.

The action freezes –

RICHARD: *(To audience.)* I say –

... I cannot deny the presence of miracle. The very essence of all life is formed from a miraculous multiplication of a single cell. The work of the scientist works several steps behind this obvious sign of something beyond science and yet –

(To audience.) I say –

…The answer may lie in brain reserve. There's a couple of scientists in Minneapolis who've been monitoring it over the past few years.

(To audience.) I say –

The action springs back into life.

It's to do with the way the brain develops in the womb and during adolescence which may lead to a stronger or weaker structure. A stronger brain may have more reserve, more grey matter. This may combat the effects of structural damage to the brain tissue, so that though the brain may have all the pathology of Alzheimers the symptoms are not displayed. These 'stronger' brains find new ways to establish connections between the nerve cells, like re-patching the wiring of a cowboy electrician, Sister Philomena displayed a high level of this grey matter. If I'm right it could be argued that she had a 'fighting' brain, may have more ammunition in 'reserve'.

RUTH: And if you are wrong? I know you're not Catholic. I mean I've never discussed it with you but I know you're not religious.

RICHARD: My mother was a Methodist.

URSULA: And your father?

RICHARD: Jew'ish.

URSULA: That will not be good enough for Ruth.

RUTH: *(Seeing URSULA's look.)* I don't understand why you don't support me in this.

URSULA: I support you in your belief of miracle, Ruth. I struggle but I support you in *your* belief of miracle.

RUTH: It's the basis of our faith, Ursula.

URSULA: Yes, and I struggle with that.

Silence.

RICHARD: Our study is exactly what it says it is, Ruth. It's a study. If we don't see it, then we don't say it's there. If it is a miracle, then no man can own it.

Distant ring of bells.

RICHARD: *'The study of mankind is man.'* That's all we're doing Ruth.

RUTH: And the study of a sister is her God.

RICHARD smiles, handing the article back to RUTH.

So we agree the jury's still out?

RICHARD: I'll do you one better. Find me a sister with a genetic link on both sides of her family to early onset Alzheimer's, who may be carrying one of the three defective genes that cause this kind of dementia and yet who's displaying no signs of cognitive failure and you might have that miracle. Now that's a pathology I'd be interested in looking at. A sister with a genetic link both sides showing no cognitive failure –

The bell passes as if moving just past URSULA's office.

RUTH: *(Beat.)* What do I get if I win?

RICHARD: You show a surprisingly mercenary edge, Ruth.

URSULA: We could do with a new television. I swear Sister Rachel has been sucking on the wires again. *(To RICHARD.)* You are so easy to wind up.

RUTH: I'll get Miriam.

RUTH exits. RICHARD lays out his things preparing to work.

URSULA: Your coffee's gone cold. Even Helen couldn't drink it.

RICHARD: You look after us so well.

URSULA: It's the highlight of our year.

RICHARD reaches for the coffee cup.

Let me get you a fresh cup.

RICHARD: Really.

URSULA: Please.

RICHARD holds out the cup. URSULA takes it.

RICHARD: I won't test Miriam if you don't want me to.

URSULA: No, Ruth is right. I'm being silly.

RICHARD: She was a little…pale.

URSULA: Ruth was saying… I know you're not meant to talk about these things but Aileen… I was wondering –

RICHARD: She was fine. The stroke had clearly been damaging but her Braak scores were fine. Everything correlated before and after –

URSULA: That's good then. That's… Only what I already thought. I mean 78. She was practically a teenager. I mean she's our first.

RICHARD: Yes.

URSULA: I can't imagine what it's like. I mean you can travel, see the world but to travel that deep into someone's mind. That's…

RICHARD: It is.

URSULA nods, returning to putting books back on the shelf. RICHARD watches her.

RICHARD: Ursula –

Distant voices.

URSULA: That'll be Miriam. Go gentle with her, OK?

RICHARD: Yes.

URSULA: I don't know what it is but… You'll see… Something's not… Something's just not –

RICHARD: It's the highlight of my year, too. Coming here? It's the highlight of my –

MIRIAM enters, carrying a radiator.

MIRIAM: You've to thank me –

URSULA: I asked Sam.

MIRIAM: It was headed downstairs but I said you need…we need it far more up here.

SAM enters.

SAM: She's like a whippet.

SAM takes it off her, moving over to plug it in.

I had my back turned for one minute and she was off.

URSULA goes to take the radiator off her, hesitating, seeing MIRIAM's nails encrusted with earth, mud on her shoes.

URSULA: What have you been doing? You've half the garden under your fingernails.

MIRIAM: I was just pulling up the bulbs. Robert leaves them to rot in the ground.

URSULA: Because they come back, Miriam if you take them out of the earth they won't come back in the spring.

MIRIAM: Now you say that but the squirrels are little monsters. It's delicious Christmas booty. I told him lay them down on newspaper in the shed and he didn't and the front bed was nearly bare this time round. I rescued them.

URSULA concedes, smiles –

URSULA: Then we are to be grateful.

MIRIAM smiles. URSULA smiles.

We were just looking over your noviciate biography, Miriam.

MIRIAM: Hmm.

URSULA: …*the sun rose through my window, casting its glorious light across my bedspread, my wall was patterned with a heavenly glow that the less rigorous minded might have taken as a sign.*

MIRIAM: Did I write that?

URSULA: Yes…

RICHARD looks up from his notes, with quiet surprise.

My preference is that I need no divine intervention for this is the start of the rest of my life.

MIRIAM: Trust in the Lord with all your heart and lean not on your own understanding; In all your ways acknowledge Him, and He will make your paths straight.

URSULA nods.

URSULA: *(Beat.)* I was just saying you haven't been well.

MIRIAM: What?

URSULA: I was just saying you haven't been well.

MIRIAM: Just a cold –

URSULA: But –

MIRIAM: I'm much better now.

URSULA: But if you don't want to Miriam, if you don't feel like being tested this morning.

MIRIAM: It's never been more important that I am tested, we both know that.

Silence.

Now where shall I sit – ?

RICHARD: Perhaps over here.

MIRIAM nods. URSULA crosses the room, pulling out a chair for MIRIAM.

Just give me a minute and we'll be ready for you Miriam.

RICHARD slides the flash cards SAM has been using earlier off the desk offering them to SAM.

A word of advice. The card tricks? *(Beat.)* Don't do them outside of the study. I've mentioned this before. It reduces what we do to a side stall show.

SAM: If I've offended –

RICHARD: You haven't. But you might.

SAM looks at the article resting on the side.

SAM: You read it.

RICHARD: Yes.

SAM: Was it?

RICHARD: It's fine.

SAM hesitates, nods preparing to set up, RUTH enters.

RUTH: There you are.

RUTH comes over to MIRIAM, starts to lay out cards in front of her, clearly preparing to begin.

URSULA: She's been outside.

URSULA squeezes MIRIAM's hands, concerned as she sits in silence.

Feel her…I'm making more tea.

URSULA makes to go.

Now is there anything else you need, Miriam –

MIRIAM: Don't fuss. There's nothing to be frightened of, Ursula.

URSULA: I'm not.

MIRIAM: Good.

URSULA nods. RUTH and SAM sit with URSULA starting work.

RUTH: Shall we begin Miriam?

MIRIAM: Yes. Begin… Yes…begin.

RUTH and SAM lay out cards in front of MIRIAM, taking notes on a clipboard as she observes –

Silence until –

Biscuit, table, airplane, handbag, dog, envelope, policeman, lake, pencil…

URSULA looking on waiting –

…and… Tambourine.

URSULA moving on.

Act Three

The library.

Later.

Distant sound of television, Newsnight or the like from a distant room.

URSULA enters, crossing the room in the half light, searching amongst the pile of documents resting on the table. URSULA hesitates, leans forward reaching for the Dictaphone. She presses play.

From the Dictaphone, HELEN's voice.

> *(On the Dictaphone.) I was born in Greenock. Though my da was a Corkman. Fifteen words. Punctuated on the sixth and the fifteenth word – End. Predominately monosyllabic bar colloquial pronoun 'da'. I was one of six. Two boys and four girls, a seventh, Michael died in childbirth. The sisters of Poor Clare were running the church school. Come fourteen, my Aunt, Tattie Pol as we were calling her, got us a place.*

RUTH enters, not seeing URSULA in the darkness. She scoops up a coffee mug, placing it on her tray.

URSULA: How's the new arrival?

RUTH turns surprised by URSULA.

RUTH: Richard's tinkering as Audrey shouts instructions from the manual. It's as thick as a brick.

URSULA: One day Audrey will be running this place.

RUTH: One day this place will be a Pizza Express and Audrey will be waitressing.

URSULA: That's not true. The World needs people like you, Ruth.

RUTH: No. The World needs fast food. And now Jonathan thinks he can butter us up, with the latest Apple whatsit.

URSULA: It's just a Christmas present, Ruth. A very generous Christmas present How long are you going to keep this up?

RUTH: What?

URSULA: This disapproval.

RUTH: Why didn't you say us? Why didn't you say 'the world needs people like us'?

URSULA: *(Beat.)* That's what I meant. Did someone drop by to check on Miriam and –

RUTH: Yes, Charlotte's reading to her now.

URSULA: I was just on my way there.

RUTH: She called me Ruthie today. She's not called me that in years.

URSULA: I am going to insist she stays in bed tomorrow. She's not thinking straight.

RUTH: Sam thinks there's a problem.

URSULA: You've talked to him.

RUTH: Yes. He's good to talk to.

URSULA looks at RUTH with a smile.

URSULA: I've seen you chatting with him.

RUTH: What do you want from me, Ursula? Some mornings I look at this place and I wonder what are we doing? For what purpose? A scrubby garden, a few classes a week, this study. I look at them sitting, growing fat, staring at the TV and I want to scream, but… I'm not tempted. I see miracle everywhere. I do, tiny miracle everywhere. *(Beat.)* It's not *me* that's lost my way.

URSULA: What does that mean? What are you trying to say? *(Beat.)* Ruth?

RUTH: Don't flutter around Richard so.

URSULA: Flutter?

RUTH: One day they'll be gone, Ursula.

URSULA: I don't know what you're talking about.

URSULA looks up; AUDREY is standing in the doorway, a computer print out in her hand.

AUDREY: We are officially online. You have a user name.

URSULA: I do.

RUTH: Everyone needs a user name to log in.

AUDREY: Aphrodite. That's your name.

URSULA: You're kidding me?

AUDREY: It was Richard's idea.

URSULA: The old fool.

RUTH exits. URSULA suddenly scoops up a book resting on the table.

Have I ever shown you…?

URSULA flicks through the pages –

Where is it? There…

URSULA pauses on a painting of the Virgin Mary.

I could look at this again and again… I love the way her face… It's luminous. Do you see?

AUDREY: Yes.

URSULA: First painting Miriam ever introduced me to. I used to sit up late and –

AUDREY: It's beautiful.

URSULA: Didn't I tell you, you had an eye?

URSULA and AUDREY silently flick through the art book.

To paint something so – All those brush strokes, it must have taken such sacrifice. It must have been so hard, when there's so much to distract –

Silence. They continue to look at the book.

Sister Aileen used to be a demon for the horses. That's what used to spirit her away. That's why we moved her to the kitchens, we couldn't trust her with the van. Right up until the end, Bernice used to count the change when it was Grand National day. 2.30 at Newmarket, that's what always spirited Aileen away. The trick is getting back. That's what we all battle with sometimes. *(Beat.)* It's a fight. I don't believe it's for you, Audrey.

URSULA closes the book, putting it back.

There are arrangements that can be made.

AUDREY: No.

URSULA: There's a small allowance that we can sub you. Just until you're up and on your way… St Margaret's still runs its hostel, and has rooms.

AUDREY: Ursula –

URSULA: No one is judging you if you don't stay.

AUDREY: Where else would I go?

URSULA: We can get you a place.

AUDREY: I won't last. I never last. Not until here. Please –

I have no one, Ursula. I'm changing. Really I am.

URSULA: Audrey.

AUDREY: I feel for the first time… Not since I was small… have I felt this…but I feel as if my blood is…I'm alive again.

Silence.

I can't leave. I can't.

URSULA hesitates, nods.

URSULA: Then the drinking has to stop.

URSULA gently holds out a hand.

We can't take you any other way.

AUDREY: I'm sorry.

URSULA: It's not a pastime. Not some well-meaning retreat. You will scream inside until your teeth ache with gritting them tight trying to hold it in some days, Audrey.

AUDREY: I want to stay.

URSULA: It's hard –

AUDREY: I'm ready.

URSULA: Sleep on it.

AUDREY: No, I –

URSULA: It's a long life, Audrey.

AUDREY hesitates, nods, makes to exit.

AUDREY: I can only try to be as good as you, Ursula.

URSULA: Goodness has nothing to do with it.

AUDREY exits.

(Beat.) God Bless.

URSULA pulls the Dictaphone out of her pocket, flicking it on once more. She listens.

(On the Dictaphone.) Predominately monosyllabic bar the colloquial noun 'da'. I was one of six. Two boys and four girls, a seventh, Michael died in childbirth. The sisters of Poor Clare were running the church school. Come fourteen, my Aunt, Tattie Pol as we were calling her, got us a place.

URSULA looks up, RICHARD stands in the doorway.

URSULA flicks the Dictaphone off.

RICHARD: It's official, I am a computer loser.

RICHARD stands, pulling his reading glasses off, a computer manual in hand.

Satan's tract. Shall I burn it now or later – ? Jonathan is definitely trying to earn his place up there.

URSULA: Sam says the sisters in Aberdeen were given a minibus.

RICHARD: Sam doesn't know what he's talking about.

URSULA: He promised me he'd swim.

RICHARD: It's freezing. *(Beat.)* You swim too far.

URSULA: You watch me?

RICHARD: You should swim closer to the bank.

URSULA: That's for pussycats.

RICHARD smiles. URSULA smiles.

Will you thank Jonathan. It's very kind, but we don't need gifts.

RICHARD: It's Christmas, Ursula.

URSULA: Still.

RICHARD: You give us so much of your time.

URSULA: Our charity knows no bounds as long as it's after *Midsomer Murders* and before *Newsnight*.

Distant murmur of a television.

Sometimes I think if it was a toss up between watching telly and… Put it this way it would be quite a squabble. My greatest fear in this world is to be left, the last nun standing, remote in hand, shouting quiz answers at the TV screen.

RICHARD laughs, clocking the Dictaphone in her hand.

RICHARD: Helen shouldn't have left that out. *(Beat.)* She's worried you don't like her.

URSULA: Helen? I like her well enough.

RICHARD: I see she's right.

URSULA: It's not that I don't like her it's just… Her analysis is very harsh. She talks about brain reserves… I mean I'm no scientist but to insinuate that the brain has a better chance of survival depending on our education, on the quality of our early lives – Some of these biographies, were written… were written…by sisters who could barely read, let alone write when they first arrived.

RICHARD: It's not definitive.

URSULA: But a sharp brain is a healthy brain?

RICHARD: It's like any muscle. A little exercise can't do any harm.

URSULA: So what do you say to a sister like Charlotte? She can make pastry as light as a feather but ask her about the state of the current economic climate… It could be hurtful to those sisters, to those sisters who haven't worked their minds in the same way.

RICHARD: Do you have fillings?

URSULA: You know I do. I smile, and a ring of steel. We can't all have braces when we're young.

RICHARD laughs. They look at one another, enjoying the moment.

RICHARD: There are a couple of scientists in Michigan who are convinced that the mercury in your average filling can seep into the brain and may be a trigger for Dementia. Then there's aluminium in coke cans. A predilection to cannabis? That won't have helped those cells much. All theories. No positive confirmation yet. A hundred and one different theories, nothing proven yet. *(Beat.)* That's why I don't answer the phone.

URSULA: Now cannabis I've never tried.

RICHARD: You really should.

URSULA hesitates. RICHARD smiles wickedly.

I'll sneak some in next time.

URSULA: How were Miriam's scores?

RICHARD: I can't discuss –

URSULA: Richard.

RICHARD: There is some decline.

URSULA looks at RICHARD.

….Some significant decline.

URSULA: Right… Right…

RICHARD: Ursula –

URSULA: If Miriam's mind is going there is no hope for any of us.

RICHARD: You have nothing to worry about.

URSULA: I'm Geraldine? 1971? You read it. You know I'm...

Silence.

…Geraldine…Geraldine Mary Louise Thomas Grey Hague if one is to be absolutely correct. Though don't ask me why. My mother had a couple of sisters who died young so I know that's why I ended up with a couple of them but… Miriam gave me the name Ursula but Geraldine is my Christian name.

URSULA flicks on the Dictaphone in her hand.

(On Dictaphone.) Tattie Pol said I must. My ma's mind was gone and my da's was close behind.

URSULA flicks off the Dictaphone.

URSULA: You've found your perfect case.

Silence –

Why else do you think I was curious about your work? I put my file out for you to see.

RICHARD takes the Dictaphone from her.

RICHARD: You're not dead yet.

URSULA: Both parents.

RICHARD: I could take a swab.

URSULA shakes her head.

It doesn't mean you'll carry the gene.

OK so maybe the odds are stacked a little higher. It might mean –

URSULA: Your study is more important to me than you think. *(Beat.)* If Miriam… Miriam had the best 'fighting' brain I know. Miriam, if Miriam can't survive this then… There is no one with a brighter mind.

She had a cold in September, it moved onto her chest. She stayed in bed for weeks. She stopped reading. I noticed a change when she didn't want to read anymore. And the laughter… There was always laughter here. She always led the laughter.

RICHARD: She could be depressed. That can cause some distraction.

URSULA: The black dog gets us all, but that's not Miriam. You and I both know that. It's like slowly being evicted from your own life.

RICHARD: It's a pretty Godless place.

URSULA: If it's Godless, we might as well all renege on the lease. If Miriam can't survive it –

RICHARD looks at URSULA waiting. She stops herself.

RICHARD: Your life here. This place –

URSULA: Could do with a lick of paint.

RICHARD: Your love and dedication to this place shines brighter than anyone could ever ask for.

URSULA: Audrey is the first intake we've had in fourteen years.

RICHARD: That's very difficult.

URSULA: Ah well. She's surprisingly committed to building a life with us.

RICHARD: Is that fair?

URSULA: What do you mean?

URSULA looks at him a sudden tension hanging –

RICHARD: I'm sorry –

URSULA: It must be very surprising to you that a young woman would want this life –

RICHARD: I'm sorry. I stepped out of line.

URSULA: You're Jewish. To you Jesus was just the son of a carpenter with big ideas.

Silence.

Now I've stepped out of line.

RICHARD: *(Beat.)* It comes through the mother's line.

URSULA and RICHARD look at one another. They laugh.

URSULA: There is no justice if Miriam –

RICHARD: It's nothing to do with justice –

URSULA: *Her* faith shone –

The distant ring of a bell, passing just outside of the office.

…shines.

HELEN enters. RICHARD and URSULA pull apart.

HELEN: Sorry, Laura was on the phone. I said I'd get you but –

RICHARD: I'm coming –

HELEN: She hung up.

RICHARD: Right.

URSULA: You should – Tonight, it's very cold…I'll…You should all, you should all have –

URSULA makes to go –

…hot milk.

URSULA exits. Silence.

HELEN: Did you talk to her?

Silence.

Richard?

Silence.

Ursula's file?

Silence.

For God sake. Can we use it?

Silence.

RICHARD: She's not in our age bracket.

HELEN: Both parents, Richard. She shows no cognitive decline. Yet. Admit it you. You are excited.

RICHARD doesn't move.

RICHARD: No.

Silence.

HELEN: Jonathan called. Edinburgh have been onto him again. You need to copy in Sam, Jonathan's already told you.

RICHARD: He's been bleating again.

HELEN: Sam's just ambitious.

RICHARD: And too young for you.

HELEN: *(Beat.)* This from the man whose wife was at high school with my cousin –

RICHARD: I know what I'm talking about.

HELEN: He's brilliant. *(Beat.)* He's got a brilliant mind.

RICHARD: Yeah, and a job waiting for him. I read his article.

HELEN: This is our fourth year, here Richard. Jonathan wants answers. None of us are getting any younger. Sam's just getting a feel for what's out there.

RICHARD: Like endorsing the next magic pill? *(Beat.)* It's corrupting and gives false hope.

HELEN: But blind faith is OK? *(Beat.)* Four years here and nine years before that in the US? That's thirteen years. We could be publishing our findings.

RICHARD: We have nothing conclusive.

HELEN: Even though there is something in what we're finding Richard.

RICHARD: We don't need that kind of press yet.

HELEN: *(Beat.)* Jonathan wants you to go to the Zurich conference at the end of the month. Go Richard.

RICHARD: And say what? That there are things we still don't understand? There are mysteries of humankind that I have no answers for at this current time.

HELEN: We understand some stuff. You could say we understand some stuff – A little flashy piece in the Sunday broadsheet would do us no harm.

RICHARD: About how some dopey Beagle has barked at a picture of a bone that he couldn't recognise last week until that shot of God knows what in his butt got him thinking for a five second dog minute?…Yeah, you're right, that wouldn't be too hard, maybe slip the sisters a quick shot of something. *Dr Richard Garfield recommends* – 'After one spoon of '*I can't believe you've got your brain back*', Gloria can now name eleven types of vegetable a minute instead of ten.

HELEN: Sam didn't write that –

RICHARD: No? But I bet you some schmuck will read it, that's $500 dollars in medication for a month that some poor desperate fuck has to shell out.

HELEN scoops up the last of the papers.

HELEN: I thought it was a fine piece.

RICHARD: Well you're fucking the guy. You would say that.

HELEN: Where did that come from?

Silence.

RICHARD: I'm sorry. That was. I'm sorry… *(Beat.)* If you're happy, then I'm happy.

Silence.

HELEN: *(Exits.)* You should talk to Laura.

SAM: Hey Richard.

SAM enters, looking over some paperwork, smiling on seeing him.

Those pathology reports.

RICHARD: I'm still going over it.

SAM: Only I really would like to compare those Braak scores, so –

RICHARD: Yeah, I'll go over with you later.

SAM: Thank you.

RICHARD makes to exit. He suddenly stops.

RICHARD: Sam, are you leaking our results to Tycon?

SAM: Sorry?

RICHARD: They make aspirin, the contraceptive pill, some of the AZT stuff, the CX516 compound you like to push so much?

SAM: I don't like what you're inferring.

RICHARD: They call. I don't pick up.

SAM: Whatever desire I may have –

RICHARD: Are you?

SAM: *(Beat.)* No.

> *RICHARD makes to go.*

Is it so wrong to want a little more, Richard? To want to share what we're finding here. I wrote an article, no shit and you can be as angry as you want Richard, but I think what pisses you off the most is that you didn't get there first.

RICHARD: I'm a scientist not a journalist, Dr Parker. Unlike you, I'm in it for the long ride. I don't presume I'm going to find answers. It's the act of asking the questions that I believe in.

SAM: Is that why you've agreed to write a book? Good on you Richard. Get a book out before they cut your funding because they will. If we don't start to translate what we are finding here they will move on to some other research programme, to someone who's got the balls to convert their findings into some kind of conclusion, Richard.

RICHARD: So they can use it to licence the next miracle cure?

SAM: Maybe.

RICHARD: Bad luck. We're not there yet.

> *HELEN comes back in, clearly something forgotten.*

RICHARD: You shouldn't leave all this stuff out –

> *RICHARD hands the Dictaphone to HELEN.*

HELEN: I'm sorry, I just –

> *HELEN hesitates, hands the file to him.*

At least think about it Richard.

> *RICHARD hesitates, exits.*

SAM: So it went well then? He won't use her.

HELEN: He won't even ask her.

SAM: So it's true then.

HELEN: What?

SAM: Haven't you noticed the two of them?

HELEN: She's a nun for Christ's sake Sam.

SAM: So was Maria… Have you never seen the movie?

HELEN: Ursula? No.

The distant sound of a bell passing as lights go out –

SAM: I wouldn't be so sure.

SAM sidles up behind HELEN as she tidies away her things. She slaps him away but he pulls HELEN closer, and starts to kiss her, pushing her up against the wall, her resistance slowly turning to laughter. The giggling subsides, as they fall into a passionate embrace.

HELEN: Have you no shame.

Through the half light of the corridor, URSULA stands, a cup of hot milk in her hands. She stops, hesitating for a moment before stepping back into the shadows, watching –

SAM: I leave that to the sisters.

The slam of a book as it falls to the floor from one of the shelves. HELEN looks up. URSULA has gone. A cup of warm milk, resting on the table, HELEN looks to SAM. SAM hesitates, picks it up and drinks. They exit. URSULA steps out of the shadows.

URSULA: *(To audience.)* If you go to the Sint Jan hospital in Bruges, and visit the old hospital infirmary, it's not in use anymore, but… You will come to the shrine of St Ursula. It's a gilded wooden reliquary in the shape of a small chapel with a saddle roof. Pinacles, gilt goblets, croquets, tralery and tromp l'oeil. But what catches your eye are the six panels painted by the Flemish Master Hans Memling denoting the journey of the young Ursula. From Breton Princess to religious martyr –

I am not a lover of Flemish art.

The first panel shows Ursula, arriving in Cologne, the second in Basel, the third in Rome. The fourth denotes her…I can't remember but the fifth and sixth are the most memorable. In the fifth you have Ursula refusing to denounce her Christian faith to Julius leader of the Huns. Around her stand the ten virgins who have accompanied her on her pilgrimage to Rome, each one representing one thousand other virgins that have also journeyed, a constant at her side for an audience with the Pope.

10,000 virgins, that's some boat.

In the sixth Ursula dies. A thin white whippet sits at her feet. It represents fidelity. Dogs always represent something. The King of the Huns, rebuffed by Ursula and angered that she has given herself to God, shoots her straight through the heart. She's got the most beautiful golden hair, twisted in braids, facing her fate, the last of her virgins still around her, hands splayed. Yes…

URSULA absently flexes her fingers.

…accepting her death. *(Beat.)* If I'd been her I'd have taken the train.

It sticks with you. There's a sister in Cardiff who sent me it on a Christmas Card. I dislike it with a vengeance. It's very …cold…Flemish art. But still. There are 759 schools and churches with the name Ursula worldwide. …My favourite are the Poor Virgins of St Ursula, a sorry group of ladies somewhere in Bangkok who do little conversion but a lot of dancing on tabletops. They were on television. Some of the sisters talk about it still.

Ursula. It's not a perfect fit.

Mary, you're safe with Mary. Angela or Bernadette? I like both of those. But 'Ursula'? Why give me a name like Ursula?

'Because she did not step down.'

There are life's natural heroes and then there are those who prefer to run, when challenged, when truly challenged. I tell myself that faith is all we have if we are to be truly strong. *(Beat.)* I stand before my fourteen now and I think of her. Her hands splayed accepting…

I want to run. I want to –

The distant ring of a bell. URSULA exits.
Interval.

Act Four

The Refectory.

JONATHAN stands lent up against a table, a plastic cup of champagne in hand.

A wide window, the late afternoon sun, shuttered out behind blinds.

An old television on a stand to the left.

A vase of snowdrops, in a jam jar on the table.

It is early spring, two years on.

JONATHAN: Sister Hilary was amazing.

URSULA: She wiped the floor with them, she really did. Didn't she?

URSULA, RICHARD and JONATHAN stand drinking champagne in plastic cups.

RICHARD: Undoubtedly.

RUTH enters.

URSULA: Ruth you had to see Hilary. I said 'you're not nervous.' 'Nervous, I'll have him for breakfast.' Have you taken her some tea?

RUTH: *(Nods.)* She's lying down. *(Eyeing URSULA.)* Are you wearing make-up?

URSULA: You have to wear make-up. On the camera, make-up is obligatory. Even Richard –

RICHARD: *(Beat.)* Just to take the shine away.

URSULA: It was fun, Ruth. Really good fun. Doesn't Jonathan look smart in his new suit?

JONATHAN: My wife warned me you put 10 lbs on on the TV screen. I thought dark might be better. As a scientist one is not prepared for public outings in front of the media. But we are modest people, Ursula we really are. Albert Einstein was well versed in his achievements. When people would ask what he did he would answer 'I changed your life.'

RICHARD and URSULA smile.

Quite brilliant. She was… Really…Hillary. Really Ruth, she is wasted on crochet.

URSULA: Don't bother. Ruth disapproves.

RUTH: Ursula.

URSULA: She fails to see that we are reaching out to a whole world of different people, a wide audience that…we never meet.

RUTH: No. Exactly. We don't meet. But we pray for and we think of and we live our lives for. We don't need to go out and court the world, to tell them what we're doing. They'll find us soon enough.

URSULA: Is everyone sitting down?

RUTH: Well… One or two haven't quite grasped the concept that you can have been interviewed this morning and already be on television by late afternoon. The sisters were worried you wouldn't be back in time.

URSULA gives up on her search, returning to pouring more champagne.

URSULA: Have they all got a glass at the ready?

RUTH nods.

RUTH: Helen's agreed to sit with those in the nursing wing.

URSULA: That's very good of her.

JONATHAN: What has this place done to that woman? There was a time she wouldn't babysit a cat, now she's reading bedtime stories.

URSULA goes to pour some more champagne in RICHARD's cup. He waves it away.

URSULA: Richard was fantastic. Wasn't he Jonathan?

JONATHAN: Made for the camera.

RICHARD: They ask such dumb questions.

JONATHAN: 'So you're actually telling our viewers that those sisters who have done something with their lives, who haven't sat around all day praying, who've stayed active and on the go, they may hold the answer to preventing this debilitating disease?'

I was floundering. Quite frankly floundering but you... Marvellous... The Erroll Flynn of the scientific world... 'I'd rather talk about the study in process. Our data is throwing up certain trends, similarities and correlations with our work in the US but I don't feel that we can positively confirm anything yet.'

We had an eight minute slot, that's longer than most of them.

URSULA: Tell Ruth how many viewers.

JONATHAN: 4.1. /

URSULA: 4.1 million viewers. Could we ever get better publicity? *(To RUTH.)* One young woman watching that –

It's life changing.

RUTH: Yesterday they had a woman on discussing training dogs for police dramas and a lady who had just won some prize for... I don't know for quite what. The point is what?

AUDREY enters. She is wearing plainer clothes, a cross around her neck.

JONATHAN: Audrey –

AUDREY: Dr Lees –

JONATHAN goes to greet AUDREY.

JONATHAN: I've not seen you since –

JONATHAN goes to pour AUDREY a cup of champagne, she declines.

AUDREY: October last...I've been away on teaching leave.

RUTH: We have a mission in Ghana.

JONATHAN: That's wonderful. Wonderful.

AUDREY: It's all on our website, you should look it up.
(To URSULA.) Miriam's gone off again.

URSULA: She'll turn up. *(Beat.)* She always does.

AUDREY: Sister Charlotte is very disapproving of the alcohol. She's taken to her room and refusing to do the Angelus at supper.

URSULA: Charlotte is disapproving of Easter eggs and Maria's Don McLean CD. It's barely a thimble in each cup.

RUTH: I'll talk to her.

AUDREY: It's not just that.

RUTH: One or two of the sisters are worried that your interview might reflect badly on them. Those like Charlotte and Margaret in the garden.

RUTH: The study's findings do point to the fact that those sisters who have not led perhaps such academic or intellectually rich lives –

AUDREY: That's not what's bothering Charlotte.

RUTH: I spoke to her, to insinuate that they have less of a chance of escaping this disease. For many of these sisters, the implication that –

AUDREY: Charlotte's not upset about that. She's read that... she's concerned, she has a brother in Toronto. Since her diagnosis she's afriad that he might worry that he has inherited the same gene.

JONATHAN: There was that question…

RICHARD: APOE gene has three variants. Sister Charlotte's DNA has shown no sign of any such gene. Her Alzheimer's is not inherited. Her brother's fine. *(Beat.)* I'll talk to her.

AUDREY: That's not the only question they have –

RICHARD: I'll talk to all of them.

JONATHAN: Let's hope they cut that bit.

RICHARD: *(To JONATHAN.)* This is why we don't go on TV.

JONATHAN: Don't be ridiculous, Richard. Really it is false modesty. You write a book, you have to promote that book. You have to go on TV.

URSULA: Lets not get dramatic. Audrey, you lead the Angelus tonight. We'll let Richard talk to Charlotte and after supper, we will talk to the rest.

JONATHAN: You do newspaper articles.

RICHARD: I don't like doing those either.

JONATHAN: Well if it bothers you, Richard, you better brace yourself, this is only the beginning.

AUDREY: That's what Sam said.

RICHARD: Sam's here?

AUDREY: He's down with the sisters, now.

RICHARD: How long has he been?

AUDREY: He arrived after lunch.

RUTH: You should see the car.

URSULA: Tell them we'll be down in *(Checking watch.)* ...a minute.

AUDREY and RUTH exit.

JONATHAN: *(To RICHARD.)* He was giving a paper in St Andrews I mentioned if he was passing by… Richard, it's time to let this one lie.
Tycon wanted to see the book, I take it as a good sign if they sent Sam. I've asked the publishers to send over a box of the first print run. They should be here, by, certainly by the end of the day. Your funding cannot last forever, Richard. We have to explore other avenues. And even if it just reminds those who have been giving us money then it does no harm.

RICHARD: No. No. I don't agree. With any of it. Today, yesterday, you invited someone from Tycon here?

JONATHAN: Not just anyone. Sam has been a loyal member of our team.

AUDREY: Ursula –

AUDREY enters, carrying a prayer book.

I was thinking I might read one of the Acts with the Angelus…The Act of Self-Dedication.

URSULA: Nice choice.

AUDREY searches through her book as URSULA recites.

Take O Lord and receive my entire liberty, my memory, my understanding and my whole will. All that I am and all that I possess you have given me.

RICHARD listens, pausing as he does battle with the DVD player.

I surrender it all to you and to be disposed of according to your will. Give me only your love and your grace, with these I will be rich enough and will desire nothing more. Amen.

URSULA catches RICHARD watching her.

JONATHAN: That was beautiful.

URSULA: Yes.

JONATHAN: Would it surprise you to know that I was once an altar boy?

URSULA: It would surprise me.

JONATHAN: My mother had great plans for me. Science was always second best.

URSULA: I never knew that.

JONATHAN: I've never really been able to get a handle on the belief bit to be honest. I go for the smells and bells but – It's the silence that always got me. At least with science there's always something to do, something to give you the illusion that you're heading towards something. My mother could furrow her brows for hours in holy conversation but I –

I admire people's faith, I really do. I'm not even lapsed. You have to actually believe in something and I never have. No voice in my head, no divine experiences. Rationally I can weigh up that there is something out there but – It's just not scientific.

URSULA: And there's the rub. *(Beat.)* Where were you married, Jonathan?

JONATHAN: St Matthew's, Canterbury near my wife's family. I know, I know. Smells and bells. That's what I like.

URSULA: Then does it really matter? *(Beat.)* I've never found him that big on conversation.

URSULA smiles, RICHARD smiles. URSULA exits.

(As goes.) Don't miss your big moment.

RICHARD: Have you any idea what some of these women have wrestled with participating in this? How many have prayed and struggled with what it means to give? We come into this world, in tact, whole and we hope we'll leave it that way. For every sister who's signed up, there is another who has not. I have never asked a sister to defend her reason. In turn I have never felt the reasons to defend my own. *(Beat.)* Until now. So I'll go on your daytime TV show. Maybe even do the odd broadsheet. *(Beat.)* Do I want my face on *Rolling Stone*? I'm not a rock star. I'm a scientist. Yeah, we can be as brutally ambitious as the next man – I do it because yeah, I can't deny knowledge, because it's addictive trying to unravel it all. But do I want to be on. 'Richard and…whatever'? *(Beat.)* I'll leave that to you.

JONATHAN: You know, you really must do something about this shyness. It's not useful in a scientist.

RICHARD: I always saw it as part of the job description. A certain insularity. I think that's what Laura called it amongst the other 'irreconcilable differences.'

JONATHAN: That's not what I hear.

RICHARD stops, turns around, faces JONATHAN.

Ursula must have been very touched by the dedication.

RICHARD: *(Beat.)* She's not read it yet.

JONATHAN: I'm not the best person to talk about marriage. God knows it's not been easy. But I'm still with the same wife.

RICHARD: There are advantages. /

JONATHAN: Richard.

RICHARD: I can eat whatever I like now. Leave towels all over the floor if I want to.

JONATHAN: The first time I met my wife was at a dinner party, nothing particularly eventful. No weird coincidences or stray acts of elaborate fate. I've always felt a little cheated about that. Other people have their stories but we…we just met and got married. It felt like the right thing to do. There are days when I know that my wife does not desire me. There are days when I look at her and ask myself why didn't I take a taxi alone that night? But here we are, forty years down the line. I could no more survive without her than Ursula could survive outside. She will never leave here. Like it or not, Richard, some of us are in it for life.

RICHARD hesitates, sinks down in the chair he has been carrying.

I hope you don't think I'm being too direct. It's only because I like you both so much. And one can always have friendship. In another life there are any number of women I might have married but I didn't. I married my wife.

RICHARD nods.

Sam is going to talk to you about some trials. Nothing too scary, just vitamin supplements etc. It would fund us here for the next two years. We will have been here over seven by then. Some marriages don't last that long. I'd take any offer very seriously Richard.

RICHARD: Two years. That won't even scratch the surface of what we're finding.

JONATHAN: Then we cannot support you any more Richard. *(Beat.)* We're cutting your funding.

RICHARD: I published a book Jonathan.

JONATHAN: With a final chapter that still does not give any definitive answer.

RICHARD: And you think two more years funded by Tycon will do what? – …Mean we can say their product works.

JONATHAN: Yes.

RICHARD: I will not be corrupted or pressurised by a drugs company –

JONATHAN: You are a brilliant scientist Richard, but you should know by now, it's also about being a brilliant businessman. Think about it. What else are you going to do?

JONATHAN makes to go, passing HELEN just entering.

HELEN: No one can find Miriam. Robert's taken the van. I would have gone but I am half a page from the end of 'Daniel Deronda' and the sisters are on the edge of their beds.

JONATHAN: A little bird tells me you have been reading to the sisters.

HELEN: I even crochet some visits. And when it's hot, I've been known to swim.

JONATHAN: I have yet to be converted but maybe if we come again in the summer then.

HELEN: I will hold you to it.

JONATHAN exits.

JONATHAN: *(Calling back.)* You're missing your big moment.

RICHARD: She can't have gone far.

HELEN: I just don't get it with Miriam.
For a mind to have been clearly so brilliant.

RICHARD: Brilliant minds do decay.

HELEN: I flatter myself I have an instinct.

RICHARD: A brilliant young mind may not sustain the course that's all. She's 88.

HELEN: I think it's depression. Depression is –

RICHARD: A symptom, not the cause.

HELEN: I was going to say as corrosive.

RICHARD: Between 15 and 40% of Alzheimer's patients we can track are depressed. It's chicken and egg. You wake up in the morning…you don't where you are.

HELEN: This is a woman who has kept her mind in the health of an Olympian. She should have a fighting brain.

RICHARD: So at best she's depressed.

HELEN: I just think it's sad. Aren't nuns meant to be radiant? I mean doesn't this life have a secret that we all want to hold. It's beautiful and all. You know it is terrible but I really hope it is Alzheimer's because if it's not and she is just depressed then what hope is there for anyone.

RICHARD: It's got to you.

RICHARD smiles –

This place has got to you.

HELEN: No… Yes…I like it…I like coming here. It gives me… hope.

RICHARD follows her gaze out of the window.

HELEN: But all those fields and trees and all that –

HELEN looks out.

…nothing.

RICHARD: Yes.

HELEN: I don't know if I could live with that but I want to believe that they can… That comforts me… That somewhere there is goodness…happiness. Peace…
A merry heart doeth good like a medicine but a broken spirit drieth the bones. It's from Proverbs… One of the nuns was reading it.

HELEN looks up, URSULA stands in the doorway.

HELEN: Miriam still missing?

URSULA: We normally get a phone call –

From far off the ring of a phone –

…about now. She'll be fine. 'Daniel Deronda'… Still?

HELEN: Half a page and I've hated every minute of it.

URSULA holds up a copy of RICHARD's book.

URSULA: Well, now we'll all have something new to read.

RICHARD reaches to take it.

URSULA snatches it away.

URSULA: This is hot off the press. There's a box downstairs, waiting to be signed but I thought –

URSULA searches for a pen, holding it out for RICHARD, opening the book for her to sign but something makes her stop, her gaze falling on the inscription inside.

…I'd get in first.

HELEN makes to go.

RICHARD looks to URSULA.

RICHARD: It's only –

URSULA instinctively raises her hand, to silence him as she reads until –

URSULA: 'For Ursula with love'.

URSULA closes the book, busying herself.

RICHARD: I'm sorry. I should have told you I was.

URSULA shakes her head, tears starting to fall down her cheeks.

You're crying. Why are you crying? It wasn't meant to make you cry.

RICHARD searches for a handkerchief, rifling through his pocket.

URSULA: It's the champagne. Really. There's a reason why nuns shouldn't drink.

RICHARD gives up his search, helpless.

RICHARD: I have a sleeve.

URSULA: A sleeve is… Good idea.

URSULA wipes her face with her cardigan sleeve.

RICHARD: It's just a silly inscription. I can have them take it out. The next press run –

URSULA: No. *(Beat.)* It's –

RICHARD: Really I can.

URSULA: Thank you.

URSULA and RICHARD look at one another, the silence hangs.

URSULA: I couldn't find my toothbrush this morning which of course is worrying particularly as it turned up in my sock drawer but –

RICHARD: I didn't mean.
There is a compound called CX516 that is being developed by the drugs company Tycon. Sam is working for them now. It's not appropriate for you now but it may be an option at a later date.

URSULA: Richard –

RICHARD: There's also vitamin supplements that I think we should be thinking about.

URSULA: Miriam wouldn't talk to me this morning. I sat with her for an hour and she didn't say a word. Just stared out of the window. At least she was talking last week. I mean not much but…I don't know what to do with her. I don't know what to do if she is not coming back. *(Shrugging.)* The other night I heard Miriam in here eating breakfast, quarter to three in the morning.

RICHARD: Ursula –

URSULA: Ruth has been trying to get Miriam to take communion. She's refused it every day. Not to accept his sacrifice, that would be enough to drive me out of my mind.

RICHARD: It won't happen like that.

URSULA: Dribbling cornflakes down my chin at three in the morning...

RICHARD: It won't change the – .

URSULA: Don't.

RICHARD: ...It won't change the way I –

URSULA: You're a kind man but...I can barely function as it. Anymore decline and –

RICHARD: No. I won't listen to that.

URSULA stops, overwhelmed suddenly, the silence hanging between them.

I like our walks.

And our letters?

URSULA: You're a very good... You've been a very good friend to me, Richard.

RICHARD: I live on the fourteenth floor. It's a very small apartment. I have a bedroom, a small study, the kitchen's not a lot to write home about... There's a park, it's not very big, it backs onto a car plant but... It's nice, it's pretty green – I've never lived there with anyone else... I rented it out when Laura – She didn't like the wallpaper. *(Beat.)* She said it made her want to cut her throat. It's about two blocks from a good deli and there's an Italian place I go to Sundays... I like pasta, I've always liked pasta, it's the one thing I cook OK.

URSULA: Right.

RICHARD: Is right a good sign? *(Beat.)* When it's late, and if it's a quiet night, the intersection gets buzzy in rush hour, I can hear the conversation of my neighbour, she's a singing teacher... 84... Sometimes, she sings bits of...I don't know... It's in some kind of language, it's very... I like it... *(Beat.)* Come back with me.

URSULA hesitates, laughs –

I'm serious. Look at this place –

Silence.

URSULA: They'll be waiting to talk to you. You know how excited they get.

RICHARD: Is that a yes or a no, Ursula?

RICHARD slides the book across to URSULA.

I wrote it for you. *(Beat.)* Think about it.

URSULA does not move, the proof of the book resting between them.

RICHARD: It would be something to tell the grandchildren.

RICHARD makes to go, leaving the proof of the book on the table. URSULA does not move. JONATHAN enters.

JONATHAN: Richard, please, they're close to chanting for you if you don't get down there immediately.

RICHARD picks up the last chair, exiting.

JONATHAN: Sam's here.

JONATHAN crosses the room.

URSULA: Lovely.

JONATHAN: I opened another bottle. I hopes that's alright.

URSULA: That's it I'm not letting you drive home tonight.

JONATHAN: I'm hoping to get Richard plastered.

URSULA: Good idea.

JONATHAN: He's a little sore. We've cut his funding.

URSULA hesitates –

URSULA: What?

JONATHAN: I know. But we simply can't support this project if he doesn't accept Sam's offer.

URSULA: Sam's offer?

JONATHAN: Tycon want to fund the study. He's going to have to say yes. Otherwise –

URSULA: What – ?

JONATHAN: He's a fool. He's coming up for retirement.
This kind of opportunity won't come around again. Even science has its prejudices. We're all getting too old. And men like Richard, they are nothing without their work. You have to talk to him.

URSULA: Me?

JONATHAN: You can persuade him, Ursula. If anyone can you can.

URSULA: When did you tell him this?

JONATHAN: Just now.

URSULA sinks into a chair.

He's reeling a little, but he'll be fine. The most important thing is he doesn't do anything rash. He's a hopeless romantic, Richard but truth is it's all about the pursuit with Richard never about crossing the finishing line. It's the essential tension of Richard's life. I do admire that but unfortunately the rest of the world just want a few certainties –

JONATHAN smiles at URSULA.

…in this strange and difficult world? You more than anyone must understand that. Your faith remains so central in the face of the unknown. It makes one feel better to know there are people like you, places like this in the world.

JONATHAN looks at URSULA, with a look of silent understanding…

Ursula?

URSULA: Yes.

JONATHAN: Thank you.

Silence. He exits.

The sound of someone on the approach, URSULA turns thinking –

URSULA: I –

URSULA looks up to see MIRIAM standing in the doorway with bare feet. She is in some disarray.

You've got no slippers on.

URSULA gets up, approaches her.

Your nightdress it's all…

She leads her over to a chair and sits her down, starting to rub her feet.

You know how wet the grass gets. *(Beat.)* Never mind, never mind…let's…like blocks of ice… Here…

URSULA continues to rub MIRIAM's feet. Silence.

Is that any better?

URSULA looks at MIRIAM's hand.

You've been gardening again.

MIRIAM: The bulbs –

URSULA: I'll get Robert to replant them.

MIRIAM: Give them back to me now, I'm not a fool.

URSULA: No one is saying that you are, Miriam.

MIRIAM: Back and forth, with that spade, turning over the earth, when there really is little point. Aileen was the only one who loved that garden. Someone needs to tell the poor man to give it up and we can just let it go. It's gone, Ursula. It's just all gone.

URSULA: No Miriam.

MIRIAM: Can't I see it with my own eyes? Don't I see it every day, Ursula.

URSULA goes to comfort MIRIAM. MIRIAM suddenly pushes URSULA away.

Will no one listen to me anymore? Will none of you just please?

URSULA: We're listening, Miriam. We're all listening.

MIRIAM: Then why can none of you hear what I am trying to say. That this place, that this…place is… It is time that this place…

URSULA: We just did the carpet, Miriam.

MIRIAM pauses, looking down at the carpet.

We chose it together.

MIRIAM: We did.

URSULA: Yes, red…you said that… Physicians used to drape it on the bodies of those with smallpox in the seventeenth century. The colour

MIRIAM: …drew out the blood, like meeting like

MIRIAM calms, sinks into her chair a little.

You wanted ochre but I said orange. So we settled on red.

URSULA: Yes.

MIRIAM: I hope they didn't overcharge.

URSULA: No, Miriam. They did us a very good deal. The underfelt was half price.

URSULA touches MIRIAM's forehead.

You're very hot.

MIRIAM: I'm very frightened.

URSULA drapes a blanket around MIRIAM, taken from a chair.

URSULA: It's alright. You sit for a while.

MIRIAM: Difficult. My breath.

Silence.

URSULA: Audrey's going to read the Angelus tonight. She's a good girl. The first evening I did the Angelus it was Easter and you made me learn the Regina Caeli in Latin and recite it in front of all the sisters when you knew I barely had spoken a word before then.

URSULA pulls the blanket tight around MIRIAM.

She slips in and out of consciousness.

If you want to go out, I can walk with you. Another month and we could go as far as the weir. It's still pretty iced up in parts but when it gets the sun –

Silence.

I swam only yesterday. Sometimes when I'm wading in through the reeds, and it's ten below zero even I wonder if I'm a little mad. Maybe I am. *(Beat.)* Am I mad, Miriam?

Silence.

I don't think I am. *(Beat.)* It would be nice if you said something.

Silence.

Finally I have got Audrey doing the VAT… I just thought I can't let Ruth go and muck them up again… I keep telling her, 'don't put Cherie down as a vatible expense because she may do the sisters hair lovely but we can't get money off it.' *(Beat.)* You know Ruth. Her maths is – You made me good at mine.

Silence.

You missed us on the telly, can you believe that? I could ask Audrey to read the Regina Caeli this year. What do you think?

Silence.

Maybe I will ask her. She's panned out quite well. When she puts her mind to it, she's really a very strong-willed girl.

Silence

I didn't make her stay.

Silence.

This is a difficult life. It's lonely. There is often little reward. You pray and you pray and you never know if your prayers are answered because people don't often ring back and say thanks. *(Beat.)* I did tell her, I made it clear. *(Beat.)* Because you never told me that.

Silence.

The absence is hard.

URSULA bends down, close to MIRIAM taking her hands.

The absence of nothing is hard.

URSULA squeezes tight on her hands.

Miriam?

MIRIAM's breathing is heavy.

Can you hear me?

URSULA grips tight on MIRIAM's hands looking her straight in the eyes.

Why didn't you tell me how hard it was?

URSULA grips tighter onto MIRIAM's hands, twisting them, tighter and tighter until –

(Struggling.) Remember, *O most gracious Virgin Mary, that never was it known that anyone who fled…your protection, …implored your help, or sought your…intercession was left unaided…O Virgin of virgins, my mother.*

URSULA slowly starts to cry, her hands still clenched around MIRIAM's hand, hurting her.

To you do I come, before you I stand, sinful and sorrowful. O Mother of the Word Incarnate, despise not my petitions, but in your mercy, I fly unto you…in your mercy, hear and answer me.

MIRIAM slowly looks down as URSULA sobs into MIRIAM's lap, loosening her grip.

There is no God. You didn't tell me that.

URSULA cries, MIRIAM gently, places her hands on URSULA's head until –

And I hate you for it, Miriam. I hate you, hate you, hate you.

MIRIAM's hand gently slides, her body quietly slumps, her breath growing heavy as URSULA looks up slowly realising –

RUTH: *(Calling through.)* You missed the whole thing, Ursu –

RUTH enters, freezing on seeing –

URSULA holding MIRIAM in slumped embrace.

Act Five

The Refectory.

Dawn. The next morning. Early morning light just scissored through the blinds –

JONATHAN sits smoking a cigarette and drinking coffee. RICHARD stands leant up against the window, a coffee in hand.

JONATHAN: This could be awkward. You try not to admit it to yourself, but I find myself drawn to the tiny pulse of a vein, the fleck in an iris…the beyond, but one is rarely…I have never been here. Only as I'm here – The last batch, there were concerns, they weren't as well preserved as they could have been –

RICHARD: …She's not dead yet.

JONATHAN wavers, goes to speak.

JONATHAN: Very true. *(Beat.)* Deserved. *(Long beat.)* But as I am here –

RICHARD: You're a viper.

JONATHAN: I'm a realist. And a neurologist and I have an interest. There were concerns that the formalin was out of date.

RICHARD: I have seen fourteen of the donations made from the UK convents, three were from here and they arrived fine. I have no complaints. The pathologist is very good. The funeral home very obliging. We don't need to piss them off. They know how to do their job.

JONATHAN: *(Beat.)* You don't have to stand before the board. We have the giants of the pharmaceutical companies desperate to get into bed with this. Not just Tycon. I had an interesting call from Zanden only yesterday, keen to do some anti-inflammatory trials on the sisters in –

RICHARD: You're a whore, you really are.

JONATHAN: It does no harm to flirt.

RICHARD: No you are worse. You pimp us out. You make us all into whores.

JONATHAN: Grow up, Richard. Take the money. Stay in your lab. One day you may just get some kind of a result.

RICHARD: Fuck you!

RICHARD and JONATHAN look up. SAM stands, drying his wet hair, an air of affluence to his dress. He smiles.

Silence –

JONATHAN: So she got you at last.

SAM: Ursula? No. She had me a couple of years ago. The trick is to get up early. When the mist is hanging low and it's just you and a moorhen gliding through. I needed that.

SAM holds out his hand to RICHARD.

Hello Richard. We didn't get to see you last night after –

RICHARD: I had some work to do in my room.

SAM: You sure know how to talk to the sisters. They were enraptured.

JONATHAN: And after that TV appearance.

RICHARD: Oh yes.

SAM: Your book sales will be up 20%.

RICHARD: All royalties go straight back into the convents.

SAM: I'm impressed.

RICHARD: I wrote it for the sisters. They get little funding and you've seen the state of some of the buildings.

SAM: That's one more slate on a very expensive roof.

RICHARD hesitates. JONATHAN heads out.

JONATHAN: I need some coffee.

JONATHAN exits.

SAM: It's very good. Chapter seven, particularly.

RICHARD: *(Beat.)* It needs one or two tweaks –

SAM: Yes, but, on the whole.

RICHARD: *(Beat.)* It's hardly definitive. I'd need more than two years.

SAM: So Jonathan told you – ? Are you going to accept?

RICHARD flicks his cigarette out of the window, making to go. SAM stops him.

Richard, what is the problem? The money was shit, the hours…you know the hours, they were just not conducive –

RICHARD: Science isn't like baseball, you don't get to do it just for the weekend.

SAM: This is interesting. What I do is interesting?

RICHARD: What? A drugs rep?

SAM: You're still pissed off at me.

RICHARD: No, I'm not pissed off.

SAM: You're still pissed off.

RICHARD: Trying to replace you was a headache for months. Ruth is pretty trained up now and Audrey's very good keeping it all in line if we need her – So if I am a little… short with you… We miss you, Sam… You were…you could be very good –

SAM: They made me an offer.

RICHARD: We could have made you an offer.

SAM: Have you seen my car?

RICHARD: You needed a car?… We could have got you a car.

SAM: They treat me very well. I feel I'm doing something. They give me a lot of respect.

RICHARD: I thought it was all that stuff you'd been leaking to them over the years.

SAM laughs. RICHARD laughs, shrugs, suddenly defeated.

SAM: I'm getting married.

RICHARD: My commiserations. I'm not the best person…

SAM holds out the packet of cigarettes to RICHARD. RICHARD takes one.

SAM: Come on…give me a break. *(Beat.)* We're on the same team.

RICHARD: Yours have nicer shirts.

SAM: We can be on the same team.

RICHARD: I don't like match fixing.

SAM hesitates, holds out a lighter. RICHARD takes it, lights his cigarette, hands it back to SAM.

Does Helen know?

SAM: She went back to George.

RICHARD takes a seat.

Any news?

RICHARD shakes his head.

RICHARD: The doctor's with Miriam now.

SAM sinks down in his seat.

SAM: You don't mention which convent the sister is from? *(Beat.)* Chapter seven, it's different from the rest of the book…I mean it's all insightful, it's all a very good analysis of the study but…I don't know exactly but something in the way you write that chapter… It's almost…tender. A sister, with both parents potentially carrying the APOE-4 gene? If we could get her signed up to one of the trials. The data on that could be very interesting to us.

RICHARD: No.

SAM: You won't even consider it? Fuck. Fuck. Do you know what I have done to get this deal in place with this study? Do you know the hours I have spent trying to translate to the goons at Tycon what your research means?

RICHARD: You left the study, Sam. That's as much as you get.

SAM: Tycon would make their gratitude clear. All we're interested in the effects of vitamin supplements on the sisters.

RICHARD: I won't rush this, Sam. I won't. I don't care how much it's worth to you, or Jonathan or Tycon. The last trial was disappointing. I won't endorse anything –

SAM: But if it would help Ursula.

RICHARD freezes, he hands back the proof of the book to SAM.

The sister is Ursula. I'm not stupid, Richard.

RICHARD: Helen told you. If this gets out to anyone, then that is it.

SAM: I'm saying nothing, but you've got to admit…

RICHARD: Back off, Sam.

SAM hesitates, throws his hands up, concedes.

SAM: You have to at least admit there is something pretty magical here.

RICHARD: Magical.

SAM: Sister Ambrose, Sister Loretta… That sister in Missouri…I forget her name –

RICHARD: Philomena.

SAM: All of them, their MMSEs scores going out of the roof and yet they're opened up and…the brain is a mess, they would have been lucky to string a sentence together let alone remember their name. Aren't you curious, that there is an answer in that? I mean these sisters, they have got something we want and when we find it –

RICHARD starts to laugh to himself.

RICHARD: We?

SAM: I wonder sometimes how interested you are in finding a cure for this. You deliberately block any intervention, any genuine desire to capitalise positively from the work here…I think you're scared, because the pharmaceuticals might get ahead, might just get that answer first and then you're fucked. Sure, you'll get a nice pat at the odd convention, but God help us they find some actual way of stopping Alzheimer's. It'll be the miracle pill they'll be praising, and you'll be left with nothing, just this gaping hole in your empty life, Richard, with nothing to fill it.

RICHARD: That is such crap.

SAM: You keep spitting out your tired tirade as much as you like, Tycon is a big company, there are other studies we can do without you. Because when we do find an answer –

RICHARD: It's that you might *not*, that's what worries me, you little prick. That you might *not*.

RICHARD looks up to see HELEN, holding a book and her reading glasses.

HELEN: How lovely, you two, as ever, getting along so well. *(To SAM.)* You look –

SAM: Thanks.

HELEN: …fat.

RICHARD smiles, HELEN smiles.

That was cruel. But it felt good.

SAM: How's George?

HELEN: What can I say? George got new glasses. They knock years off him.

SAM: I'm sorry.

HELEN: I missed the cat.

HELEN goes over and feels the pot, pouring the last dregs into his cup.

This coffee's shit. *(Beat.)* Did the doctor –

RICHARD nods.

RICHARD: He's been with her since four –

HELEN checks her watch.

HELEN: Ursula was very, not herself, there was such despair… Ruth thought it was the champagne. It doesn't agree with me either. Still…

URSULA enters, her reading glasses and the proof of the book in her hand.

URSULA: You're getting eggs. They could be scrambled or poached or fried, Charlottes's sneaked into the kitchen again. Audrey's been trying to ease her quietly out for the last six months, but somehow she always slips her way back in. If you don't let her, she mopes around the place like a neutered cat. Whatever, you'll get something.

HELEN: You look exhausted.

URSULA: I'm fine. I tried to get some sleep at about six but… It gave me the chance to catch up with my reading. There is the funniest scene in the kitchen. Jonathan is attempting to make his own coffee. Charlotte is grinding the bean. It's Nescafé but she's trying to convince him it's real.

HELEN: Any word on.

URSULA: No. *(Beat.)* Ruth's with her now. She wanted Ruth. *(Beat.)* It's a very strange thing watching someone die. It's a slow fade. The breath gets very shallow. I've opened the window. I'll go back in a minute but I just –

JONATHAN enters, carrying a pot of fresh coffee.

What time did you get to bed?

URSULA takes in SAM and JONATHAN, their general dishevelled attire.

No?

SAM: The sister's had us playing whist.

URSULA goes to pour herself a cup of coffee.

URSULA: If you've lost money I've no sympathy.

URSULA spills some, the cup shaking in her hand.

RICHARD: Let me do it.

RICHARD pours her a cup –

URSULA: The mist… It's hanging like a gauze over everything. *(Beat.)* This is my favourite time of the year. Aside from the fact it is my birthday, my true birthday, March is a very optimistic month, filled with signs of the resurrection.

URSULA drinks her coffee.

I've called the hospital. They'll pick her up soon after I presume it will be as it was with Aileen and the Brody sisters? *(Beat.)* ...One or two of the sisters don't think you actually take anything out. There's been much heated debate over the years, but the best one put forward was by Hilary who said that you follow the hairline. *(Beat.)* I always worry you might get them mixed up.

RICHARD: We try our best.

URSULA: Because I was thinking – *(Beat.)* I don't want you to take Miriam's. *(Beat.)* I'd rather you didn't.

JONATHAN: Ursula –

RICHARD: No decision has to be made –

JONATHAN: She's signed the consent form.

URSULA: I'm unsigning it.

JONATHAN: You can't do that. Miriam's wishes are clear –

URSULA: And I'm saying no. She doesn't need to be prodded and poked any more.

JONATHAN: You've been such a supporter.

URSULA: Yes.

JONATHAN: May I ask/

URSULA: Don't keep persisting Jonathan, or I'll know you've been visiting for more than just our company.

JONATHAN hesitates.

JONATHAN: I'll have to call the office.

JONATHAN exits.

URSULA: Helen, Ruth was asking if you might read to Miriam, she might want a few minutes relief.

HELEN: Yes of course. Right.

HELEN exits.

URSULA: *(Beat.)* I can't actually do it, can I?

RICHARD: No.

URSULA: I thought not. Then I'm asking you. Please don't take her brain.

RICHARD: She's not –

URSULA: No.

RICHARD: So there's no decision to be made yet –

URSULA: *(Beat.)* How much did you lose?

SAM: A couple of… Twenty pounds… Sister Bernadette said it was for/

URSULA: It never goes in the blind box. You need to get better at cards.

RICHARD: Sam do you want to go and check on –

SAM hesitates, nods, understanding.

SAM: Sure.

SAM exits.

They sit in silence until –

RICHARD reaches out to URSULA, the cup of coffee awkward in his hand.

URSULA: You're spilling your coffee.

RICHARD curses, wiping the stain from his shirt.

It'll stain.

RICHARD: So it stains.

URSULA: Just dab it with a bit of water.

RICHARD: It's fine… Don't fuss, OK.

URSULA: Champagne…does not suit me.

RICHARD: Ursula –

URSULA: Do you know the painter Grünwald?

RICHARD hesitates –

RICHARD: You sent me those tickets, I meant to go…

URSULA: He was German. Sixteenth century. A bit of a mystery. I mean there are doubts as to whether he even existed. But a number of paintings… One painting, of Christ, The Crucifixion, has been attributed to him. It's very unusual because – You really should try some religious art.

RICHARD: I liked that picture of Mary by the cross…

URSULA: It was on a biscuit box you gave Ruth, last Christmas –

RICHARD: They were expensive cookies.

URSULA: Honestly Richard you have no shame…

While the Italians were painting altarpieces of luminous beauty, Grünwald supposedly painted it as it was. Christ is gaunt, palm strained, wounds seeping, Mary weeping at his feet, begging for him to be brought down. And all around the sky is black, apocalyptic. *(Beat.)* It terrifies me but…I used to make myself look at it, tell myself anyone who painted this must know that God exists. He must be sure that the Son of God did come down and that he died for our sins. It comforted me. Next to it Grünwald has painted the resurrected Christ. He's glowing and magical and omnipotent. He's saying… Look one has to go through such pain, such martyrdom, because there's the promise of eternal life. It's a lie…I see now it's a terrible lie… It's propaganda of the worst kind. 38 years I've lived by this lie. This place gets harder the older you get. You start with verve, you feed that verve. You read, you absorb, you learn. You set yourself challenges; you do all you can, believing that somehow it will bring you closer to him. Often I didn't. I have not believed. What saved me is that Miriam did, had the best 'fighting' brain of anyone I have ever known. She would question. She would challenge this. She would encourage me to discover more, to find an answer, but the truth is… Knowledge just takes you further away. It's the darkest place.

But that does not mean I can leave.

URSULA holds the book in her hand, holding it out to him, to give it back.

Faith must remain because it cannot be proven.

Silence.

Thank you. It is a beautiful book.

Silence.

Take the money, Richard.

RICHARD: Did Jonathan – ?

URSULA: Take the dirty, filthy, corrupt and beautiful money. It will buy you a couple more years.

RICHARD: I –

URSULA: Take it. This is what I am.

URSULA holds out the book to him once more.

It's what you are.

AUDREY: *(Calling out.)* Ursula –

RICHARD takes the book from her. AUDREY enters, a copy of the morning newspaper and a pot of coffee in hand.

AUDREY: We made the papers. *(Reading.)* 'West Coast sisters hold key in "contemplative" life.' *(To RICHARD.)* Charlotte's done you breakfast.

URSULA: I'll swim before mine.

AUDREY: Third column.

URSULA looks over AUDREY's shoulder at the paper –

And a photo.

URSULA looks up and sees RUTH –

URSULA: Has she – ?

RUTH nods.

RUTH: I'm sorry.

URSULA suddenly cries. Sudden. Shocking. Like an animal.

ALL: Hail Mary
Full of Grace
The Lord is with thee
Blessed art thou among women
And Blessed is the fruit

of they womb, Jesus.
Holy Mary
Mother of God,
Pray for us sinners now,
And at the hour of death.
Amen.

…letting the tears slowly subside until –

RUTH: Ursula –

RUTH reaches out to touch URSULA, comfort her.

I'm sorry. She didn't know what she was saying at the end.

URSULA: She called out for you. She wanted you. I'd want you too.

SAM enters eating a piece of toast.

SAM: *(As enters.)* They're talking about taking her to St Peters –

RICHARD: Shut up, Sam.

URSULA: It's fine. It's fine. Why else are you here? If you wanted to follow, Robert could take the van –

URSULA makes to go, RICHARD stops her.

Please Richard, let's not…this is why you are here. This is why you come here. To this place, to this shitty little decaying corner of nowhere, nowhere that we have tended and loved and believed in…believe in… How do we believe in… How do I believe in…now…without without…

URSULA sobs, until she is laughing, sobbing and laughing.

I'll swim first.

URSULA makes to go.

RUTH: Shall I call –

URSULA: They're standing by.

SAM: *(Beat.)* I'm sorry.

URSULA: You've butter on your cuff. Samuel. Where did you steal that suit?

SAM: My fiancée… I think… *(Reading label inside the jacket.)* Hugo Boss.

SAM absently wipes as URSULA goes over to the window, drawing back the blinds –

URSULA: That's lucky, he must be the same size as you.

A sea of snowdrops, just visible through the window. URSULA considers, exits.

AUDREY: I'll go and keep an eye out for the –

AUDREY hurriedly exits.

RUTH: *(Calling out.)* Tell Anna Maria, I've laid out her habit and veil –

AUDREY has gone.

Is there any left in that pot?

RICHARD nods, going to pour RUTH a cup.

I better go phone Miriam's family. She has a cousin in Vermont. Please don't worry about Ursula. I know you will but. She's always been more dramatic than the rest of us. Miriam called it her 'artistic' mind. But it will pass. It will come to pass.

RICHARD hands RUTH a cup of coffee. She drinks, following RICHARD's gaze out of the window.

RICHARD: She swims too far –

RUTH: *(Nods.)* Yes.

RICHARD: The reeds, she should swim closer to the –

RUTH: *(Beat.)* She will come back.

RUTH goes to clear up the coffee cups and pot as JONATHAN enters with HELEN. RUTH exits.

SAM: Is it here?

JONATHAN: Just coming up the drive. Why don't you take Helen? I can follow in my car.

RICHARD: *(To HELEN.)* You OK?

HELEN nods.

HELEN: I just read until –

RUTH exits.

You know we pick away at these women's lives and yet I never think about their dying.

JONATHAN: *(Beat.)* We should get going.

HELEN: Yeah –

JONATHAN: Richard –

RICHARD nods.

This one will be interesting…

JONATHAN finishes up his coffee and makes to go.

SAM: *(To RICHARD.)* You coming?

RICHARD remains looking out –

RICHARD: What time is it?

SAM finishes his coffee, and goes to follow.

SAM: Five past, by my watch… *(To HELEN.)* Are you coming with me?

HELEN: OK, but you keep your hands to yourself. I'm a married woman.

SAM: Yeah, yeah, yeah.

SAM makes to go, holding out his hand to RICHARD.

Richard?

RICHARD: Two years. You can have two years.

SAM smiles with surprise. RICHARD hesitantly shakes it.

SAM: We'll be in touch.

The toot of a horn outside.

HELEN: I'll push him out the door when we take a sharp bend.

RICHARD smiles. SAM exits.

I leaked the data to Tycon. *(Seeing look.)* What can I say? Love does strange things to you.

HELEN follows RICHARD's gaze through the window –

I can't see her.

RICHARD points a finger –

RICHARD: She should turn any –

RICHARD nods to himself, a sense that she has.

HELEN: Don't leave me with them too long. I don't trust those two.

HELEN kisses him on the cheek. She exits. RUTH comes in, her coat on.

RUTH: All gone? Never mind. *(Beat.)* I thought I might go with her but.

RUTH takes off her coat.

I'll be needed here. *(Beat.)* Will you be working while you're here, Richard?

RICHARD: No, I fly back tonight. We won't be back here until the fall.

RUTH: I keep threatening to go and visit our sisters in America.

RICHARD: You should come… I could do with someone to help… There's this book tour –

RUTH: Me?

RUTH smiles, surprised, makes to go, bell in hand.

RUTH: I'll go wake the sisters. Charlottes's crying into her scrambled eggs. Someone's got to eat them –

RUTH exits. RICHARD looks back, watching her.

RICHARD: *(To audience.)* In my apartment block, there is an elevator. I travel in it every day. Once in the morning, once in the evening. On occasion it gets stuck. Not for long but enough to feel the cold seep of claustrophobia. If someone is there, I front it out. Cough, adjust my tie, bend down, tie a shoelace, breathe. But if I'm alone, for a moment I lose my mind, I mean really on the edge of losing my mind and then –

That hum kicks in and we're moving again. I flirt with changing my life in that moment, turning it all on its head. In those few terrifying seconds I will be braver, I will work harder, I will live more fully. I will but then... I get out at my floor. As I do every day.

URSULA enters, dripping wet, drying her hair.

URSULA: I swear someone swallows the remote.

URSULA checks her watch, as she goes on a search for the remote control.

I promised the sisters I'd get this mended, before their quiz...

The distant ring of the bell.

When often it's just a simple case of changing the batteries.

URSULA at last finds the remote and aims it at the TV. She tries to turn it on. Nothing.

I normally nick them from Margaret's alarm clock.

URSULA fiddles with the back of the remote box.

URSULA: But today –

URSULA tries to turn on the TV with the remote. Nothing.

URSULA starts to fiddle with the remote –

RICHARD: *(Beat.)* Our study has shown at worst –

URSULA grips his hands, they look at one another.

RICHARD: *(Long beat.)* ...even in some of those sisters whose pathology in death have confirmed severe damage to the brain tissue –

URSULA resumes fiddling with the remote control.

...who may have genetic links, who were less educated, whose mother never took folic acid before birth, even in some of these sisters, we have found in life so little cognitive failure that it stuns science – . *(Beat.)* It gets lonely, that doesn't mean it's not out there.

URSULA: I struggle with miracle.

RICHARD: Well for now, I'm sorry Ursula but the miracle is yours.

From outside.

AUDREY: *(Calling out.)* Ursula –

RICHARD: We'll be back in the fall. And the year after. And the year after that –

AUDREY passes by the doorway as URSULA absently rubs the batteries in her hand, pushing them back in the remote.

AUDREY: …did you remember you were going to go over the Regina Caeli with me?

URSULA: It went right out of my head.

URSULA tries the remote again. Suddenly the TV comes on, some inane morning TV quiz –

AUDREY: *(As goes.)* Even if you forget him, he won't forget you, *(Calling back.)* I'm struggling with the Latin…part.

URSULA: You'll love Latin.

AUDREY's gone. URSULA stands watching, remote in hand. The action suddenly freezes.

RICHARD: *(To audience.)* There is a gallery I visited on my honeymoon. It was raining and I remember my wife and I ran in just to get away from the damp and the misery. We stayed for over an hour. My wife was… To be frank, I am not an art lover. She wandered, cooing and smiling, delighting in every corridor. I went in search of coffee.

Standing in line at the cafeteria, there was a painting; it was just above the central door. I remember it struck me. I was drawn to it straight away. I can't even remember the artist. David something… I'm not good with names. I tried to buy a postcard. I looked on every rack. They'd run out. It was obviously a popular choice.

A monk is standing on shore looking out over a wide sea. It's not exactly stormy, but it's threatening and yet there is light. Seeping through the clouds, not in biblical proportions but enough, just feathering the darkness. The monk is tiny, a spec on the sand. I think his arms are out.

When I returned to Chicago, that was where we were living at the time, I tried to get hold of it but –

Life has drifted on, my marriage is long over, we even have a new president –

It is August, yeah August, and I have just come in from work. It's late and I've picked up a take out. The fan on the air conditioning has broke again. It's like an oven this time of year.

On the door mat is a postcard. I recognise it straight away.

Monk on the Seashore

Casper David Friedrich 1774-1840.

'Sticking close to the bank as I can. Saw this and thought of you. He was big in the German Romantic movement. See you next year. Ursula'.

On the TV screen –

A hostess is standing before a row of letters. The action suddenly springs back into life.

URSULA: Here we go. Here we go.

Suddenly the picture shifts on the TV. URSULA goes forward and slaps it. RICHARD smiles, watching URSULA.

RICHARD: *(To audience.)* Miriam's brain was…there were signs of degeneration… It confirmed what I thought… Obvious Alzheimer's… But you don't die of it… Pneumonia, that's what killed her… Pneumonia got her in the end… Ursula never asked to know…and I never told her. The pathology of a sister is for her alone and… It's a very private affair.

Some nights, when I am sitting in the lab, holding up a slide to the light, I see the wonderment of life in a flash, the tiny plaques and tangles that carry the mysteries of *us. (Beat.)* Ursula comes to mind. It is often late, and the last technician is just checking out. Somewhere in another place –

URSULA: Psephology P.S.E.P.H.O.L.O.G.Y.
(Shouting at the TV screen.) That's easy…that's easy.

RICHARD turns to look at URSULA.

RICHARD: *(To URSULA.)* Let's get you a new TV.

URSULA: Huh?

URSULA goes back to watching the game show. RICHARD watches her.

RICHARD: *(To audience.)* It keeps my faith.

URSULA stands, remote in hand, in front of the TV.

URSULA: *(Shouting at the TV screen.)* Come on, you can do it.
Ten letters, from the Greek.

From the TV screen, some inane answer.

It could be worse.

The babble of the quiz show.

Lights fade on URSULA as she stands, remote in hand.

The End.

WWW.OBERONBOOKS.COM

Follow us on www.twitter.com/@oberonbooks
& www.facebook.com/oberonbook